X-RATED

TO

G-RATED

LIFESTYLE

AN AUTOBIOGRAPHY BY
KANDI ROSE

Shepherd's Rose Publishing

Hot Springs Village, Arkansas

Copyright © 2005
KANDI ROSE

All rights reserved. No reproduction of this book in any form, such as electronic, mechanical, photocopying, recording or stored in a retrieval system etc. without permission. That permission must be in writing by the author or publisher.

LIBRARY OF CONGRESS CONTROL NUMBER: 2005901046
ISBN: 0-9766197-0-9
First Printing   May   2005

To PURCHASE additional copies or to CONTACT the author KANDI ROSE, write:

SHEPHERD'S ROSE PUBLISHING
P.O.BOX 8780
Hot Springs Village, Arkansas 71910-8780

Send check or money order in the amount of $16.00 per book (includes tax, shipping and handling). Make it payable to: **SHEPHERD'S ROSE PUBLISHING**
Please allow up to 3 weeks for delivery.
KANDI ROSE is not only an AUTHOR, but an EVANGELIST as well. The country outfit, sheep and staff on the back cover are worn for illustrated sermons. Call this number if you feel God would have her come speak to your congregation to reach the Good Shepherd's Lost and Wounded Sheep.
1-800-436-7082 enter 2506097 to leave a message
www.shepherdsrose.com

Printed in the U.S.A. by Morris Publishing
3212 East Highway 30
Kearney, NE. 68847
1-800-650-7888

Edited by: Mark Haston
Formatting done by: Bridgett Graves
Photography by: Bill Carpenter

TABLE OF CONTENTS

CHAPTER 1 **DADDY'S DEMONS**
INCEST AND DECEPTION

CHAPTER 2 **A VICTIM OF RAPE**
FROM BEING USED TO USING OTHERS

CHAPTER 3 **I BECAME PORNOGRAPHY**
NUDE MODELING / KIDNAPPED

CHAPTER 4 **A CHEATING HEART**
BETRAYAL AND PROSTITUTION

CHAPTER 5 **THE HOMEWRECKERS**
ALCOHOL, DOMESTIC VIOLENCE, ADULTERY, PORNOGRAPHY AND GAMBLING

CHAPTER 6 **DIVORCED AND DESPERATE**
FROM STRIP DANCING TO OWNING A STRIP BUSINESS

CHAPTER 7 **THE CHOICE THAT AFFECTED MY DESTINY**
VICTORY OVER EVIL!

FOREWORD

This book will help many. I am so happy she put her experiences to words.
 - **Dan Vukmirovich**
 Production Director / Victory Television Network (VTN)

I have known Kandi Rose for over 20 years. She has appeared on my show, "CROSSROADS", twice. The best description of my dear friend and sister in Christ is, GOD'S Grace. She's madly in love with Christ and radiates His love.
She has something to tell the whole world. It will break your heart, change your mind and bring you into the SHEPHERD'S PRESENCE.
 - **Rita Marcowitz**
 Television talk show host / producer and author

"If you want a real life picture of the triumph of God's grace over the power of sin, then you need to read this book. Kandi's story will make you laugh and cry as she vividly relives her life of extremes. Her story is not an easy one to write, as Satan had many strongholds in her life for many years. You will feel the hurt of her heart as she candidly includes the details of so many devastating effects of sin. Today, she has a victorious testimony of God's power to heal and restore. Kandi is a modern day Rahab who was taken from the depths of sin to the heights of God's grace. This book will compel you to reach out to those around you with addictions, and it will challenge you to renew your commitment to God."
 - **Mark Haston**
 Senior Pastor, Hot Springs 1st Assembly of God Church

APPRECIATION

To My Good Shepherd / Jesus Christ
You not only FOUND ME as your LOST SHEEP, but you have given me meaning and purpose in life. Thank you for your great LOVE, FORGIVENESS and POWER. I LOVE YOU SO MUCH! Thank you for The HOLY SPIRIT'S wisdom and inspiration to write this book. I don't take credit for this as I know this is one of those many miracles that you love to do. I am your **ROSE!**

To Dan Vukmirovich:
Production Director / Victory Television Network (VTN)
Years ago God told me there would be a book written about my testimony, telling of His LOVE, FORGIVENESS and POWER. I always thought someone else would author it. Prior to this book becoming a reality, you Dan, spoke words of encouragement and motivated me to sit down and undertake this task. This miracle took place about two weeks after our conversation. Under the guidance and inspiration of THE HOLY SPIRIT, I sat for hours, every day, non-stop, until it was done. This was SUPERNATURAL, AS I DON'T EVEN LIKE TO WRITE LETTERS. My mom would tell you, I call, not write her. God used you to give me confidence that, **"THIS WAS THE TIME, TO DO IT."**
Thank you Dan for being led by THE HOLY SPIRIT!

To Millie Bryant:
Author of, "A Chainsaw And A Shovel". The Dennis Hamilton Story (Rescue mission for men)
I attended the HOT SPRINGS VILLAGE AGLOW meeting where you and Dennis ministered. This was about a week following my conversation with Dan, from VTN. God gave you and Dennis a message from the WORD OF GOD that confirmed to me again that I

needed to write this book. You called me out for prayer and I KNEW, THAT I KNEW, it was, "**FOR SUCH A TIME AS THIS**". **Thank you Millie and Dennis** for being vessels of THE LORD!

To Mark Haston:
Pastor of Hot Springs First Assembly of God

Thank you for volunteering your precious time and talent to edit this book. You're so busy not only as a Pastor but Missionary as well. Yet you chose to do this labor of love as unto The Lord. You've been God's extended hand many times to my family. You visited my previous husband in the hospital and then partook in the funeral service. When God put Daniel in my life, you married us. You've also been one of my Bible College teachers. **Thank you Pastor Mark,** you're a GOOD earthly SHEPHERD.

To Bridgett Graves:
My precious daughter-in-law

I love and appreciated you so much. Thank you for all of the many hours you spent to format this book to specifications on the computer. You let me use your lap top and showed me how to use it. You gave me computer lessons enabling me to take those written words and enter them as a PDF file. You too, have been God's vessel to reach the lost and wounded sheep of THE GOOD SHEPHERD. **Thank you Bridget,** you're part of THE SHEEP-ROUND UP.

To Jim and Jan Campbell:
Two of my closest friends in the ministry

Jan, when I told you I was starting to write this book, you planted a financial seed. We both cried and prayed together for this story to reach the LOST AND WOUNDED SHEEP worldwide. The Lord is going to honor you and Jim for your faithfulness. You have always shown by your CONSISTENT HOLY LIFESTYLE that you truly love JESUS. **Thank you Jim and Jan,** you are God's servants.

To Patrick and Joy Dobbs:
Christians, showing the love of Christ

Patrick and Joy, you have shown your love for Christ by your acts of KINDNESS to me. Thank you for donating your computer. It was an answer to prayer to make this book a reality. You too, have part in the Harvest this book will produce.

To Daniel:
My unselfish, loving husband

Thank you for financially giving when you could have gotten yourself a better truck, hunting gun, or bow. This is just another of the many times when you have sacrificed for us. Thank you for believing this book will reach thousands of THE GOOD SHEPHERD'S LOST AND WOUNDED SHEEP. **I Love You So Much,** you're my gift from God.

DEDICATION

This book is dedicated to my praying mom and step-dad. They not only prayed for me, but also showed me that true Christianity is a holy, loving lifestyle. You showed me unconditional love, AGAPE LOVE (God's love) through your acts of kindness. He's good and kind to us even when we don't deserve it. The X-RATED life I led was shameful but you extended to me what Christ extends - mercy and longsuffering.

MOM, you not only gave me physical birth but helped spiritually birth me as well. On March 5, 1984 you led me in a sinner's prayer on the phone and Jesus came into my heart and life. John 3:3 became a reality - I was BORN AGAIN. In spite of all your physical and emotional pain, you kept the fruit of the Spirit. When I faced a crisis I wanted what you had - JESUS! Thanks for showing me the way!

PAPA, my real dad never showed me what true fatherly (Godly) love is. You have shown Godly love to me by your consistent Christian lifestyle. You have shown acts of kindness by driving me places, moving me, giving me money, fixing things of mine, and so many other things. Jesus said, "what you have done unto the least of these, you have done unto me." I certainly was one of the least. You not only have done those kinds of things for me, but my children, and their children as well. What an example of Jesus you are. You've never had flesh and blood children of your own but you have treated all of us as if we were. Before you were healed of cancer, I saw the peace you had as well. Thanks for showing me the way!

DANIEL, you are my gift from God. I never thought I'd love anybody like my deceased husband, Donald. God is full of surprises. Nothing is coincidence or just luck. I use the terms "God hook-up" or "devil hook-up" and you definitely are a "GOD HOOK-UP". God has given us two wonderful grandchildren, Evie (age 11) and Gabe (age 12), so that we can show them the way to Jesus. Daniel, you are needed and appreciated and we love you so much. This book will have bad things in it about me. I've shared a lot with you but I pray you will not be embarrassed but happy to say, "My wife may have lived an X-RATED lifestyle but now she's living a G-RATED (GODLY) lifestyle". Thank you for giving me the time to write this! You have given me your blessing to not work right now so that I can concentrate on this book. You are so good to me. I couldn't have married a better person. I thank Jesus for you!

    LIL, you are my timid friend whom God gave the boldness to ask me to church. Thank you for your prayers and for witnessing to me. That is what Christians are supposed to be doing. Others probably just assumed I wasn't ever going to be saved since I was living such an X-RATED life. You saw a soul that needed Jesus, and just like Jesus you saw my heart - not the sinful activity. You saw what I could be for God. You were a good example by your consistent Godly lifestyle. Thank you for being my spiritual mentor as we visited many church revivals, concerts, Bible studies, etc. Thanks for showing me the way.

    BRO. JOHN, you are the special evangelist God sent to me the night before I was saved. You inspired me by your testimony since you were a former addict and gang member. I saw a joy and peace in you just as I had in my parents and friend Lil. I praise God that you came to that little church and showed me the way to Jesus.

"For the Son of man is come to seek and to save that which was lost." (Luke 19:11)

ACKNOWLEDGEMENT TO MY FAMILY

Years ago I've told each of you how very sorry I am that I embarrassed and hurt you by my old (X-Rated) lifestyle. I disappointed and shamed each of you by my actions and attitudes. I not only brought you shame but was not there for you when you needed me. You suffered from my destructive choices. I do believe that you have forgiven me, as Jesus has, and I am so grateful for that. I love my precious family members so much and value my relationship with you.

You know me better than anyone, except for the Lord, and can attest to the reality of the pages written in this book. You are all living witnesses of God's love, grace, and power to change a life. Some of you have experienced your own miracles by allowing Jesus to make a difference in your lives.

I certainly looked like an unlikely candidate but that's what God's love and the cross is all about. The Bible is all about taking sinful people and making them righteous through the blood that Jesus shed on the cross. This book is being written to tell everyone that his love and forgiveness is available to all. I'm an example of His power and mercy and great love. To those of you in my precious family who aren't saved yet, if Jesus can turn my life around – he'll do the same for you. He'll do the same for those who read this book or hear me preach. As you well know I didn't change myself - I couldn't. I tried many times to stop different addictions and inward character traits on my own. That's why this story has to be told. I am one of God's miracles. I am one of the many people throughout history who have been sought out by THE GOOD SHEPHERD. I'm one of those who have heard His voice of love calling to me and I said yes with my whole heart. I pray instead of being embarrassed you'll be happy to say, "Yes that's my daughter, mom, grandma, or wife." She may have had an X-RATED LIFESTYLE but NOW she's living a…G-RATED LIFESTYLE!

PREFACE

As a Born Again Christian now for many years, I have read the Bible through several times and have had numerous Bible College courses through Berean Bible College. Knowing what GOD'S WORD tells us, and from personal experiences, life is a SPIRITUAL BATTLE. There are UNSEEN forces of GOOD and EVIL at work trying to INFLUENCE our CHOICES. This BATTLE begins when we're yet in our mother's womb and continues during our physical life here on earth. IT IS A BATTLE between the power of GOD and the power of the DEVIL. John 10:10 says that Satan is a thief who has come to **"steal, kill and destroy"**. Satan, the devil, is real. Not a pitchfork guy, but a SPIRIT who leads many DEMONS (fallen disobedient angels) to mess with our body, mind and soul. The good news is that our lives can be indwelt by GOD'S HOLY SPIRIT when we become BORN AGAIN. The bad news is that we can CHOOSE to let the enemy use us by OUR DESTRUCTIVE CHOICES to hurt and INFLUENCE OTHERS. This book has been written so that you can reflect on what has happened or is happening in your own life and the lives of those around you (see Ephesians 6:10-18).

Our enemy hates us because we are God's creation. Since he hates God and rebelled against Him, he continually tries to DESTROY EACH OF US. He knows his destiny is Hell and he continually LIES to us (John 8:44). He tries to get us THROUGH OUR CHOICES to take us with him to hell. God loves us (John 3:16) and He's not willing that any should perish (II Pe.3:9). When JESUS died on the cross, He broke Satan's power over us. We have the POWER and ABILITY to not only CHOOSE to TURN FROM our sinful actions and attitudes (repent), but we can now live a consistent G-RATED lifestyle. The blood JESUS shed on the CROSS makes us righteous (right standing with God). God doesn't want to send anyone to Hell. He's a HOLY GOD and sin will separate us from Him on that final day. WE WON'T BE ABLE TO SAY, "THE DEVIL MADE ME DO IT."

Jesus gave His life so that we could be saved. There's POWER in the BLOOD and the NAME of JESUS CHRIST. Before I was saved, my life was an example of what happens to a LIFE INFLUENCED BY THE DEVIL. The life I live now illustrates how God can in His love and mercy and forgiveness make something G-RATED out of it.

At the end of this book there will be a prayer for you to say if would like JESUS to come into your heart. God is alive and He is a Spirit (John 4:24). You can't see Him but He is there and has been all these years. He wants a PERSONAL, INTIMATE, RELATIONSHIP with you. You are LOVED and PRECIOUS in His sight. You can become one of His sheep. Let Him take you into His fold and watch over you and guide you. Let YOUR LIFE BE USED BY HIM and not the devil. There is so much PEACE and JOY knowing you BELONG to HIM and that your life can have MEANING and PURPOSE instead of just EXISTENCE.

Please let me know if this book has touched your life. I love you, but Jesus loves you even more. Remember that God has great plans for you (Jeremiah 29:11). It's time to cancel the devil's plans! Give your whole-hearted COMMITMENT to the ONE who LOVES YOU and DIED for YOU!

Please note: Due to the sensitive nature of some of the material in this book, some of the names have been changed.

CHAPTER ONE
DADDY'S DEMONS
- INCEST AND DECEPTION -

DADDY! How I loved daddy. I will always remember his smiling face. Everybody loved daddy - his family, my mom's family, and everybody that met him. He was a family man to folks looking from the outside in. We were always doing family outings, picnics, and special occasion activities. He worked everyday. We were a low-income family who lived in rural northern Michigan for a few years, but most of my young years were spent in Chicago. I never saw daddy drunk. He just drank an occasional beer. I can't remember fights or violence in our home, but there was an EVIL SPIRITUAL force active in our home. When I became older, my mom told me of some of the sickening things that happened in secret between them.

I was a very affectionate, kindhearted little girl. My mother never had to spank me. I always wanted to please her and daddy. I was promoted in school three times back when school was a six month promotion instead of one year. I had just turned 13 when I entered the 9th grade and I got along well with other kids and shared whatever I had. Mom taught me good morals and manners. I'm not boasting - I just want to let you know what type of person and LIFESTYLE I led. I was so innocent and naive, as children should be. I had no idea that my family and I were victims of a DEMONIC force that was out to destroy our home. No one can tell me that there isn't a spiritual force behind the scenes. I've experienced that warfare as we all have. As I reflect on my life, I'm not only aware of the evil but definitely aware of the HOLY SPIRIT and angels that have intervened on my behalf.

When I became an adult, my mom shared with me that when she was pregnant with me, daddy had kicked her in the stomach so hard that it knocked her out of bed. The devil wanted to abort my young life. As a tiny baby when I was crying in the crib, he slapped me real hard in the face. Mom vowed after that to never leave me alone with him and she didn't. He never babysat me while she went somewhere. I don't remember her ever leaving me with anyone - not even family members. Little did she realize the DECEPTION and EVIL ACTIVITY that was happening right under her nose. There's something very enticing about sin, something so evil, that the very idea of almost getting caught is exciting.

One of my earliest childhood memories is of me on a potty-chair and my daddy messing with me. He performed a sexual activity on me that wasn't just touching, but yet not the actual act itself. I don't want to get descriptive in any way but that is the reality of what started happening to me from ages 3 to 11. Much of that went on, as well as touching me, and non-stop exposure of himself. Years later I realized that the evil spirit of EXIBITIONISM had become a major factor in my life.

Mom didn't get saved until later in her life. She always prayed though and taught me to pray the "Now I lay me down to sleep" prayer. Mom had a hard life herself. She grew up as an adopted child to a very elderly, affluent family. They never expressed love for her and basically used her as a housekeeper. She didn't get to hear words of love or affirmation or self-worth. Her adopted parents had a family that was already grown at the time. Two of the brother-in-laws that were adults molested her at a young age. When my future father, a migrant worker from Tennessee, came to pick cherries in upper Michigan, he met mom. Her adopted parents owned huge cherry orchards. Daddy was a likeable, smooth talker who appeared to be just the dream man for mom. I'm sure she dreamed of someone who would show her love, as she never had it in that family. Mom is a very affectionate, loving person.

Mom grew up in church, but had never seen a true Christian lifestyle at home since my grandparents weren't saved. They went to church for appearances but were never actually born again. To those that looked from the outside-in, these were good moral people. One brother-in-law and his wife were both schoolteachers and he even became the principal. He was my teacher in 4th grade. The other brother-in-law was a successful affluent farmer and owner of vast cherry orchards. Both were avid church-goers. Yet these men let the devil use their life to molest my mom. Mom could write a book herself.

Mom did have someone in her life that God placed there for her. Her Sunday school teacher who taught her that Jesus loved her. With no love from anyone else, those words were wonderful to hear. That's why people who work with children and teens are very important in God's kingdom. Their influence will impact them for a lifetime. Years later, I had the same lady for a short time. Teachers should never minimize the calling God has given them. It's as important as being behind the pulpit. My mom had not yet had a true conversion experience while I was growing up, but had great respect for God. I remember that she told me about my body being the temple of God and that no one should touch it until you're married. She had no idea what was going on in secrecy. Daddy had told me that if I told mom she'd have a heart attack and die. I'd seen her have an attack where she turned blue and couldn't breathe. It was scary and I grew up for years living in dread that my precious mom would die and leave me. So I didn't want to seal her fate by telling her this awful secret.

When illicit sex is introduced to a child, teen, or adult it becomes an evil doorway for the demonic forces. An addiction to that pleasure steps in. One thing leads to another. Since mom had taught me to pray I was aware of God. I started feeling guilty about what was going on. I know now that the guilt was from Satan, not God, as I was just a victim, an innocent child. After praying "I lay me down to sleep", I would always add "PLEASE FORGIVE ME GOD." I know now that there are countless millions of victims of Satan out there who know what I'm talking about. Those who have had similar experiences, or are still experiencing this awful demonic attack, JESUS LOVES YOU! IT'S NOT YOUR FAULT! Your victimizer is a victim themselves to Satan's schemes and needs to be saved and set free from his devices.

At about age 10 my dad tried the actual act itself. He was always so sneaky. My mom was in the kitchen and we were right outside the house by the window where she was. So praise God he wasn't successful, but all the other evil activity was non-stop for about 8 years.

When I was 11 years old I had begun hearing about sex from the school kids. I remember as if it were yesterday that one day when I got off the school bus and walked down that country driveway, there stood daddy. He was off to the side behind the shed as usual exposing himself again, grinning real big. I boldly proclaimed, "DADDY, I'M A BIG GIRL NOW - YOU'RE NOT GOING TO TOUCH ME ANYMORE!" That had to have been The HOLY SPIRIT to give me such boldness and to say it with such authority because I was always petite, meek and timid. He never touched my body after that. God must have put a fear in him that I just might tell. The indecent exposure continued daily for the next 4 years.

We eventually moved back to Chicago. It was a horrible time, and I grew to hate the sight of a man's naked body. Daddy even tried to give me money to show myself to him. One day at age 15 I'd had enough. I risked telling mom even with her health condition. Satan is such a liar. My mom is still alive today, thank the Lord! Mom and I have always been very close and I knew she loved me. She always showed her love to me by giving me lots of innocent hugs and kisses and by playing games with me. Mom always said that I was her gift from God. She'd had rheumatic fever when she was little and they said she'd never walk again. After being bed-ridden, God performed a miracle in her life and she walked. She was then told to never have children or it could kill her. So when I was born it was yet another miracle. Mom treated me as a treasure.

At age 15, I gave her news that crushed her world. I told her all about this evil abuse. I emotionally couldn't deal with it by myself anymore. Mom couldn't deal with it either. She was shocked. She had no clue. He was so DECEPTIVE. Mom cried and cried, then in anger and hatred, she confronted daddy. He denied it over and over, acting so innocent. He claimed that I was lying but mom knew better. She knew lying wasn't part of my character. She knew that if I said something, it was the truth.

Mom also knew daddy's character because of what went on behind closed doors that no one else had seen. That perfect father image was all a facade. It was hard for her to conceive he would be that evil to molest his only blood child. I respect and honor my mother still to this day for believing me. Millions of people are not believed when they reveal the dark secrets that have tormented them. Thank you mom!

She immediately threatened divorce. I begged her to stay with him and he was crying and begging too. Because I was still in denial, I couldn't bear the guilt of them getting a divorce on account of me. Mom agreed to keep the marriage together because of my hysteria. It was an awful time. After a very short time had elapsed, he began exposing himself again. I remember this scene vividly. There was no door on their bedroom that was off the kitchen, only a curtain. Mom was doing dishes at the sink and I was at the table. I turned and there he was with the curtain slightly parted exposing his self and grinning as usual. I stepped back into the small pantry and waited for mom to turn around. When she did I pointed to the bedroom doorway. She saw for herself. THAT WAS IT! We were now ready for divorce. Things got bad - daddy had a mean temper that only mom knew about. He threatened us with his army machete that he always had behind the front door. With our lives in danger, we left with only what we could put in shopping bags. Mom didn't drive and we had no car. By using a city bus we moved to another neighborhood in Chicago. She rented a 3-room apartment and walked miles to work for a cheap factory job. She couldn't even afford the money to ride the bus to work. We left all our personal stuff behind just to get away from DADDY'S DEMONS.

A spirit of depression seized my poor mom. After walking to and from a hot and tiresome job in the factory, she'd sit for hours crying. She'd sit in the dark and play those "somebody done somebody wrong songs" and bawl her eyes out. For 17 years she'd been a kind, loving, and faithful wife. Now she felt that there was no hope. My mom remained kind and loving toward me, but other evil forces came not only upon her, but upon me as well. The spirit of HATE, BITTERNESS, and UNFORGIVENESS entered our home. These are tormenting spirits from the pit of Hell that will eat away at you like a cancer. That spirit bound my precious mom for years to come until the day she became born-again and her heavenly counselor healed her broken heart.

As for me, even though I had kept loving daddy through my childhood, it was like my eyes were opened and I was filled with hate, bitterness, and unforgiveness as well. Poor me - how could he have done that to me, his little girl? Who opened my eyes to those thoughts? Satan did, of course. It was the beginning of his negative voice for many years to come. Years that led me down a path of destruction that lasted almost twenty years. Twenty years that eventually led to an X-RATED LIFESTYLE. It didn't happen overnight but little by little through one compromise after another. Rationalizing, justifying, and minimizing my actions through all my destructive choices that would follow. Always blaming, always making excuses, and always saying, "POOR ME"!

If you'd told me at age 15 I would end up living such a shameful lifestyle, I wouldn't have believed it. I was sweet and naive back then. To any teens or young adults reading this book, my eyes are filled with tears for you (my own precious grandchildren, this is for you too). Be aware there's a spiritual battle for your mind heart and soul. Turn to JESUS now! Don't let the enemy take you down a path of heartbreak, full of consequences. Don't let him waste your precious life and ultimately send your soul to HELL. There is a God who loves you and knows the heartaches you've already endured. Let him comfort you and heal your broken heart. Let Him be the love of your life, your best friend. Satan wants to destroy you emotionally and physically. Jesus has great plans for your life. He wants to take all the bad and turn it for good, so you can show others that Jesus is Alive! Your life can have meaning and purpose. God has uniquely created you with special talents and abilities so that you can help others find their way to JESUS. As I look back, I see not only the evil SPIRIT OF HATE AND

UNFORGIVENESS that oppressed me, but the SPIRIT OF SELF-PITY. They remained for almost 20 wasted years.

CHAPTER TWO
A VICTIM OF RAPE
- FROM BEING USED TO USING OTHERS -

Just prior to mom and I leaving dad with shopping bags in hand, I made some bad choices. I became influenced by older teens in high school. I started cutting classes. We were living in Chicago where I loved school and even made excellent grades. The tactics of our enemy Satan have worked for many generations. We all want to be liked and accepted so we go along with the crowd and end up with bad consequences. That's when THE SPIRIT OF REBELLION reared its ugly head. On one of the days I cut class, the principal was right outside the door and caught a friend and me. She told us to bring our parents to school. We freaked out and hopped on an inner city bus and rode it to the end of its route. We ended up in one of the worst neighborhoods. It was very scary to spend the night in a nasty hallway. We had ransacked some cars and got a carton of cigarettes from a glove box. I mentioned I was a good girl growing up to age 15, but at age 11 I had started smoking cigarettes through peer pressure. Before I was saved, I was smoking 2 packs a day. Until I got saved, I smoked for 24 years. That was another addiction from which God set me free. Someone reported us to the police and they found us hidden in a dark nasty basement. They had our parents get us at the station. We were fortunate that they found us alive and well. Those surroundings could have brought harm to us. Thank you Jesus! I hated the police at that time but now know that they are GOD'S hands extended to us to help us.

My grades went from excellent to failing due to the class-cutting. When I turned 16 I quit school. I was in the last half of my junior year. Things went from bad to worse. During this time, I got involved in a gang for a short time. I started drinking wine in alleys, sniffing airplane glue from brown lunch bags, and getting into fights with gang members. I was still pretty naive at the time and not hardhearted like I would soon become. I heard that a girl was after me to beat me up. I remember being so terrified. I made my mind up that at least I wouldn't just lie there and take it like I had before. When I saw that tall girl coming down the street with her mean-looking face, I took off my good coat. I hit her first and put her in a head-lock. From that time on, I had no more fear of anyone - even huge women or even men. I actually became a bully. I always laughed and said dynamite comes in small packages. Fighting doesn't solve anything. God says vengeance is his. I wouldn't learn this though for the next 20 years and had many more fights along the way.

We moved to another neighborhood soon afterwards, but it didn't take long for the devil to come knocking with even worse temptations. At least I was away from the gang but if there's no spiritual change you can't run from yourself. I kept making bad choices and the consequences came crashing in.

As I mentioned earlier, mom was heartbroken, worked like a dog in the factory and was very lonely. On top of all this misery I made it worse. I was now letting that SPIRIT OF REBELLION rule my heart and life. Mom was so easy-going and felt because I have been through so much, she hated to come down hard on me. She'd never had to before. I had changed from Jekyll to Hyde. Now with my dad out of the picture I DID WHATEVER I FELT LIKE. When someone has no restraints or willingness to listen to authority, FREEDOM can END UP MAKING YOU A SLAVE. I BECAME A SLAVE TO SIN. AS SATAN BEGAN TO USE ME, I BEGAN TO USE OTHERS. Use people he does. In this life you can choose to let God use your life or you can let Satan use your life. Our life and our choices affect all those around us. Our lives influence each other either for good or evil. By writing this book I pray you'll be influenced to let God use your life. It's an awesome, exciting way to live - Partnering with God and showing others the way to Jesus.

I eventually started drinking wine, whiskey, and beer, smoking pot, taking downer pills and speed, and shooting up with desoxyn. Later on in life, cocaine also entered my life briefly. I loved catching a buzz. Although there were plenty in Chicago, there wasn't an organized gang in my new neighborhood. Later on I would associate with a well-known motorcycle gang for a short time. There were many of us who hung out on street corners, drinking and fighting between ourselves. We also met with teens from all over the Chicago area for drag races (illegal ones of course between the teens to see who had the fastest car). There was a street where mostly factories were and when the police would come, we'd scatter for a short time and then return. It was a big party scene. Everything appears exciting and fun when you're young. Now I realize that even as I got older I kept seeking thrills. Look around and you'll see all ages caught up in some kind of evil, looking for fun and excitement. The Bible says, "SIN IS PLEASURABLE FOR A SEASON" - that means a little while. It never satisfies though. You're always looking for more as you keep compromising your morals to obtain pleasure. Addictions of all kinds follow that obsession. You want to be accepted but overall you end up with consequences that bring great heartaches to not only you but your family as well.

  I went to one party and got so drunk that I ended up being raped by several guys. How pitiful! Satan takes advantage of us. That's why the Bible says to not even associate (HANG OUT WITH) with non-believers. God knows that others influence our lives and we can fall prey to destruction. On another occasion I went on a date with one of the most popular guys in the neighborhood. He was 17 and I was 16. I was so excited because he appeared to be a real catch, but he ended up USING ME. In a dark garage sitting in his muscle car, a '57 Chevy, he forced himself on me. I began crying so loud and feeling so humiliated when I heard the car door open. His uncle who was in his 40's took over, threatening me and hurting me. Some people would probably say, "She deserved it". She wasn't a virgin anyway and shouldn't have been where she was. No human being should be treated like that, even a prostitute (which I later would become).

LITTLE BY LITTLE MY HEART WOULD HARDEN. It seemed like all men were alike. Later in life I WANTED TO USE THEM BEFORE THEY USED ME. When rape, incest, and kidnapping happen to you, trust is lost - Trust in people and trust even in God. Now I know that it's never God's fault when those things happen to you - it is a person's free will to choose to do evil. Just as later on in life I would learn that I, too, used my own free will to make evil choices - choices that not only hurt me but others. That's why today I can have forgiveness and mercy, not hate, toward all those I have been a victim of (including my dad). I have been a sinner and needed forgiveness and mercy. JESUS said that if we don't forgive others - He won't forgive us. Sin is sin, no matter how big or small. It's all bad in God's sight. If Jesus can forgive His persecutors that nailed Him to the cross and die for sins (theirs, mine and yours) then I can forgive also. At this point in my life, I had not yet received this Good News of Jesus. There are people in this world with similar stories to mine (even seemingly moral people) who Satan has lied to and who need the truth brought to them. Romans 3:23 says ***"ALL have sinned and fell short of the glory of God"***. Then Romans 6:23 shares with us, ***"For the wages of sin is death; but the gift of God is eternal life through JESUS CHRIST our Lord"***.

I soon met a twenty five year old man who also bought me an engagement ring. He was from a small town in Arkansas and was visiting his family in Chicago. He was the first man that with whom I had consensual sex. I was 16 and he would be the first of many. He went back to Arkansas and quickly sent me a greyhound bus ticket. I was a city slicker who looked at a sleepy little town and thought "no way, I'd be bored stiff". But I always loved the south. My daddy was from Tennessee and we had family in Missouri. At 16, the country life seemed far too dull for me. How funny is it that I currently live in Arkansas in an even smaller town! I'm a country gal now and love it. That's what Jesus can do, give you peace and contentment. Needless to say, I mailed that ring back pronto.

Soon after that short relationship I met a 23 yr old married man. I was almost 17 and he brought lots of excitement (so I thought). At this point I wasn't looking for marriage or commitment, just fun. Through the years I would find only temporary fun and end up feeling EMPTY, USED and ABUSED. Only Jesus can fill the void in your heart. The man was only at his house during the day because every single night and weekends we were together. I don't even remember feeling guilty for being with a married man. Satan can dull God's voice if you allow him. My lifestyle had HARDENED MY HEART. We continued to see each other for about a year. He was a pool shark. I had acquired a fake I.D. and met him in a country bar. I say country, because even though this neighborhood was multi-cultural, there were many people from the southern states who lived in this area. They had come to Chicago like we did looking for higher paying jobs but they usually remained in poverty. He didn't work and so gambling was his only form of income. He was one of the best pool players I would ever see. He taught me how to play and I was his partner at times. Everyone thought that they would win because I was a girl. At that time, women very seldom shot pool. So many people were willing to bet big - thinking that had a sure win. My boyfriend was so good that he made up for any of my weaknesses. As time went on, playing pool and gambling would become one of my greatest addictions and obsessions. For the next 20 years, I couldn't even enjoy the game unless I could shoot for something - which mainly meant beer or money. If I walked into a bar and there was no pool table or no one shooting, I'd go to another. I bounced to many, many bars all by myself, driven with this compulsion. I went into bad, bad neighborhoods too. I had no fear of man or woman. I walked in with such a chip on my shoulder that if you even looked at me funny I'd be ready to fight. At that time a game of pool was only a quarter and you could line your quarter on the table and count how many people were ahead of you. I was ready to fight anyone if they jumped my quarter. I saw many fights over a pool table. I once saw my boyfriend beat someone with a cue stick. When you mix booze, pool and gambling there's a good opportunity for evil.

      My 23 year old boyfriend also stole cars. I praise God we never got caught. Sooner or later the Bible says, **"*Your sin will***

find you out". So if you continue, no matter how slick you think you are, it eventually catches up with you. After about a year, I left this bad relationship and wound up with worse ones down the road.

The SELF PITY and BLAME GAME really set in and stayed for almost 20 years. The devil must have really been laughing as he continued to lie to my mind. That SPIRIT OF REBELLION gives us such a hard heart. My attitude through life was much the same of millions of teens as well as older adults. The attitude is: I'll DO WHAT I WANT, WHEN I WANT, AND NO ONE IS GOING TO TELL ME WHAT TO DO, DON'T TRY TO CHANGE ME! Even people who are much older act and talk like that - especially people addicted to something. I've "been there, done that" and almost all my male relationships have had that attitude. That's why we would fight like cats and dogs. Each person tried to be in control, while all along we were out of control. We gave the control to the devil and didn't even realize it. I am so glad that the Holy Spirit is in control of my life now.

That kindhearted sweet girl I had once been had vanished as I became full of hate, bitterness and unforgiveness. These are demonic forces that will bring great misery and destruction to your life. A SPIRIT OF REVENGE came next. You so often see this glamorized in movies and television. Everyone seems to justify revenge when someone has victimized you or your family. HOLLYWOOD MAKES IT SO EXCITING. Don't be fooled - simply ask those who've been part of it if it made them feel any better. It doesn't - it simply eats away at you.

There was two times during that 16 - 17 year old period that I had MURDER IN MY HEART. Very late one evening, after drinking heavily, I started listening to those evil spirits. It came to my mind to borrow my date's knife and get him to drive me to my dad's apartment. As I was going up that darkened stairway to the second floor, I remember having such hate well up in me as never before. I began beating furiously on daddy's door but with no response right away. Then, just as I least expected it, out he jumped and threw me to the floor. Since I was drunk I was like a limp dishrag. I remember that knife narrowly missing my own throat. I was cursing and screaming loudly when my date came up the stairs to check on me. Daddy was a chicken when it came to men so he got off me. Of course he didn't call the police. What would he say, "She's here to get REVENGE for the INCEST"? I was so frustrated so I immediately began to plan a second attempt. Within a short time I jammed a butcher knife down the waistband of my jeans, and headed out again to my dad's apartment. This time he wasn't home but a very overweight woman who was probably his girlfriend answered the door. I smacked that door open all the way, and boldly walked in without an invitation. I had a mean look, a bad attitude and a mouth full of curse words. I began demanding any items that belonged to mom and me. Since it had been a good amount of time since we had left, the woman said that daddy had thrown it all out the window in the back yard. I was furious. Then I noticed a hanging 3 D picture I'd bought mom by selling Christmas cards. I yanked it off the wall. This lady was so scared. I was enjoying being such a bully. The picture was of Jesus, who 20 years later, would become the love of my life, MY GOOD SHEPHERD.

I'm so glad I didn't succeed with those evil plots. I'd be on death row or already executed for MURDER. You know what the Bible says about murder? To even think about murder or to think about doing any other sin is just as bad as doing it. There are no big or little sins with God. We look to people in prisons and get all self-righteous. We just didn't get caught sinning whether it was in action or thought. God knows what we're thinking or doing. The prisons would not be able to hold everyone if we got what we really deserved. We are all born with a sinful nature and our own righteous morality is as a filthy rag. (Isaiah 64:6). We all need Jesus to take our sinful nature (thoughts, actions, and attitudes) and allow His Holy Spirit to come into our hearts and make us brand new and born again (2 Cor. 5:17). I'll explain more about how to do that at the end of this book. He's awesome and it's a wonderful and exciting life living a G-RATED (GODLY) life.

During these teen years and the adult years to follow I escaped death many times. Car accidents alone could have snuffed me out and I'd be in HELL right now. Once you die without being born again that's it. While you have a breath to breathe we have to make that choice. TODAY IS THE DAY of salvation (2 Cor. 6:2).

As a teen we'd hang out on street corners and wait for someone to come in a car and take us joy riding. Party, party! We always looked for someone that had not only a car but also money to buy booze. Any kind of booze or drug would do. We would even jump in with a total stranger just for thrills and so-called excitement. Several times I was in cars that drove about a 100 miles per hour trying to outrun the police on the expressway. They would dodge in and out of traffic or speed down small two lane residential streets and alleyways. On one occasion a girl who was riding in the middle front seat went berserk on us. She had a bad buzz of some kind. I was sitting in the front passenger seat next to her when she stiffened her leg and slammed her foot on top of the driver's foot over the accelerator. We were on the expressway with lots of traffic, three lanes on each side. I started slapping her face so hard and tugging on her foot to get her to release. It took a while - talk about a wild ride. Did I learn anything yet? No! We all just laughed it off. God sent His angels and I didn't even know it.

I almost overdosed on downers called "Christmas trees" one hot summer day. I vaguely remember my mom trying to get me to stay home, begging me. I gave her such heartache and grief, as if she hadn't suffered enough during those 17 years being married to daddy. I was so selfish that I only thought about POOR ME. During this incident it was about 90 degrees and I headed out to the streets wearing a heavy black leather jacket. I walked aimlessly not even knowing where I was. A stranger approached me and asked me if I wanted to go to a party. Sure, I was always interested in a party. Everything else is pretty vague except I became aware I was about to be another rape victim. I remember running and running until I ran into an apartment building. I ran up the stairway and pounded on a door until a young married couple opened the door. I told them I was being pursued by a stranger so they let me in. She let her husband take me home. Of course I thanked him but I didn't thank the Lord. I didn't know he was really the one behind my rescue. Thank you FATHER, DADDY-GOD! I know now!

    We tend to lead selfish lives before being saved. It's all about us, not recognizing the hurt and needs all around us. I could have been a real comfort and blessing to my mom. Instead I became a great thorn in her side. And not just then, but all the selfish years I would waste afterwards as I pursued happiness. During those years I'd curse her for just asking me in a mild way if I'd please stay home. I'd throw food, furniture and even scissors at her. When I got saved one of the first things I did after asking God to forgive me was to beg my mom's forgiveness with true remorse. As I bawled my eyes out to this realization, my precious mom was so compassionate and cried herself. She reminded me of what Jesus said on the cross, ***"FATHER FORGIVE THEM, THEY KNOW NOT WHAT THEY DO"***. That's what mom said basically to me. She knew the devil had blinded my eyes. Mom's love had always been there for me just as GOD'S LOVE HAD ALWAYS BEEN THERE FOR ME. I know now, and when hurts come, I allow my HEAVENLY DADDY to comfort me.

    Mom wasn't saved till much later in her life. She was always a good person. Of course she'll tell you to this day that even though she may not have done all the horrendous things I have, she knew she was a sinner and needed JESUS just as much as I did. She was so lonely and I imagine as she would walk to the corner store or restaurant she'd hear the loud country music coming out of the local nightclub. These places appear to be so much fun. People are drawn to them looking for someone to talk to and companionship. There's always someone there willing to listen, as we all seek love and acceptance. The world is full of lonely people seeking the need to belong to somebody or some group. That's why bars and gangs have no problem attracting people. The devil has his ways of offering the counterfeit of where happiness, peace, love and fun are. I know now it's not found in those places. A personal relationship with Jesus, going to church, and hanging out with other Christians HAS ALL OF THAT!

While I was going through all of the things, the same devil that was having a field day with me was messing with mom. Thankfully not to the extreme that I allowed him to but nonetheless sent my mom in the wrong direction. Mom had loved and listened to country music all those years that she'd been married to daddy, but had never been to bars. She was a good wife and mother, a homebody. I know loneliness drew her there. I certainly wasn't at home for her. She sat depressed every night crying in a darkened room. So when she did go to that club it became a habit on weekends. She'd sip vodka and orange juice slowly all night. I can never remember my mom ever previously drinking anything. Even when she started going to those bars I never once saw her drunk. She never brought men home either. Soon mom would meet the man she would marry in the future. Mom didn't realize it then but he was a gift from God to her. He is a wonderful caring man who treated my mom like a woman should be treated - with love and respect. He called her "angel" and still does to this day. He is a country man from, guess where, ARKANSAS. He became my gift from God as well. This man, by his acts of kindness, showed me he cared. We eventually grew to have a very close relationship after I was saved. They didn't get saved until years later. HE WOULD BECOME MY GODLY DADDY! Mom had a hard time believing he was for real. Trusting a man was hard for her. She kept expecting him to change. He didn't change for the worse at all. He got saved around the same time she did. GOD IS GOOD!

CHAPTER THREE
I BECAME PORNOGRAPHY
- NUDE MODELING / KIDNAPPED -

Just prior to turning 18 I met another man my age. We met at a factory where we both worked for a short time. His name was Carl. I thought I was in love. I moved in with him and his parents. We drank every night and soon lost our jobs due to drinking. We hung out on those street corners with the rest of the crowd. Since I had a fake I.D. we also went to the bars when we had money.

Carl didn't like to work, so, when a friend of mine told me about her job GO-GO DANCING I was interested. Let me explain what a GO-GO DANCER is. The costume was a bikini type with fringe, feathers or lace sewed on. This type of dancing went on in nightclubs and bars. Later in life I would end up doing a full strip. It all appeared so glamorous. Those beautiful, colorful, Las Vegas type clothing that's worn in movies and on TV. Ladies - don't let the devil sell this bill of goods to you! BEWARE you'll end up BEING USED in such a degrading way.

Well I was very excited, as the money was top notch. I had always been broke and this sounded like such a great opportunity. She drove me to her agent's office. I was impressed. Here were many young girls and women even up to their 40's primping in a large room. It was just like you'd see in the movies with the Hollywood dressing rooms - big round light bulbs surrounding lots and lots of mirrors. Plenty of makeup, perfume, and colorful sequined lacey costumes hung everywhere. I couldn't wait to get one of those costumes. They were custom designed for each dancer and cost big bucks. I soaked a lot of money into them through the years. Some were very elaborate. I would soon find out that all this would be a farce because it led to low self worth and esteem, a feeling of BEING USED. That's exactly what it is too. The devil exploits us and USES WOMEN AND EVEN MEN through this type of pornography in action. The devil doesn't care, whoever is willing, HE'LL USE.

I had stage fright at first and would close my eyes dancing. I loved to dance and when the music would start I'd let go. Now I realize that there was an evil spirit inspiring me. I ended up being such a creative dancer with a real flow of moving my hands and feet. I was one of the best. I now do a holy dance for the Lord and realize that the Holy Spirit can inspire me to worship and praise ALMIGHTY GOD. I used to dance with veils for the devil and now that creative ability is used to bring GLORY TO GOD as I dance for Him.

The SPIRIT OF GREED AND LUST came upon me, making ME LIVE PORNOGRAPHY. A HARD HEART was needed for this job and the devil had me well prepared in advance for this disgusting period in my life. Money, money, money!

The love of it is the root of all evil. You'll compromise all your morals and standards to get it. This agent had connections to clubs throughout Chicago, Old Town, Rush Street, and even as far away as Gary and Hammond, Indiana. They would pay him a commission off each of us girls so they could be insured of having dancers all the time. He even drove those of us who had no car. We'd get a flat rate, cash that night, plus commission on the drinks we could hustle from the customers. After we'd do our 20 to 30 minute show on stage we'd go mingle with the customers to get them to spend their cash and especially help run up their credit cards. Of course if you wanted to make a lot of money, you had to be a smooth talker and con artist. It was disgusting. I loved to dance and would become one of the best but mingling was the most degrading. You had to have a HARD HEART and at first I hated USING these guys like that. Then the other experienced dancers would say, "Hey, they're here to USE US, so USE RIGHT BACK". My philosophy was to take them for every penny I could squeeze from them. So needless to say, I learned to talk and act the part. I ended up working through this agent off and on through the years when I needed quick money. I figured out that I had danced at 33 clubs.

I became pregnant by Carl when I was 18 and danced until I was 4 months along. During my 5th month when my stomach had a little pooch, I was KIDNAPPED AT KNIFE

POINT. Carl and I had just gotten an apartment with my dancing money because he didn't work. In between my dance jobs we would still hang out on street corners. As usual, there were always a lot of our friends there. One of those nights became a TERROR for us that we'd never forget. A 25 year old handsome guy stopped at our corner and hung around drinking with us. We should have known he was bad news when he badly beat up an old wino friend of ours. This old guy was mild mannered and harmless. He would buy booze for those underage and they would give him a little extra so he could get some wine. This 25 Year old named Paul flew in a rage over nothing and beat him bloody. Nobody stopped it. That's the way street rules are. Nobody stops fights. I have seen people's throats slashed right on the street, almost killing them. It wasn't unusual for that type of activity to go on.

As the evening wore on, there were only 5 of us left. We were with another couple our age and the girl was 5 months pregnant just like me. It was getting late and we didn't want to be hassled by the police. They were always cruising by causing us to scatter. So, we invited these 3 people to our apartment.

After a short time I heard crying even though our stereo was on real loud. It was coming from the bathroom. I noticed this guy Paul and my girlfriend were not in the living room. Only Carl and her boyfriend were there. I thought this was strange so I knocked on the door and heard muffled crying. I began to beat on the door and cursing this guy Paul to come out. A few minutes went by and out he came and ran into the living room and ordered her boyfriend to hit the road. Hit the road he did, as he was a coward. He was afraid of this older guy who was very tall and muscular. Then Paul went back into the bathroom with her and locked it. Well I was furious, I knew what it was to be raped and since she was pregnant it was even worse. I banged harder and harder cursing as loudly as I could. We had no phone and I guess I thought I was bad enough to handle it - not so. This guy was yielding himself big time to the DEMONIC SPIRITS. You can't judge a book by its cover. This guy didn't appear to be evil by his natural appearance.

Carl was 6' 2", just slightly taller than Paul but was no match for this older, more muscular man. Carl took a butcher knife from the kitchen to protect himself but Paul took it away. Then he ordered Carl, my girlfriend, and I into the living room and ordered us girls to disrobe. I was cursing him but he threatened to kill Carl if I didn't. My friend could not stop crying because of what she had just been through. We were both pregnant and this was so humiliating. Suddenly, Carl jumped up from the couch and headed out the second floor back door. We quickly put our clothes back on and by the time we hit the outside front door, there he was, grinning. He told my girlfriend to hit the road. He grabbed my arm tightly and jerked me down the street, threatening me with that big butcher knife. I was screaming and cursing and trying to get out of his grip but he made me realize he was crazy enough to kill me. So I shut up at that point and that's when I realized I was alone and in real danger. TERROR started to set in. It was just he and I now and I felt really alone and deserted. I look back now and know that I wasn't alone - God and his angels were with me or I wouldn't have survived to write this book. I was barefoot and we walked and walked through alleys and gangways until we came to his grandma's house. He didn't let her see the knife but I knew it was there, so I did as he said. He was there to get money. Carl had called the police and looking back as a Christian I know JESUS rescued me. When Paul realized the police were there, he opened the second floor window. He made me get out onto the roof of the next-door apartment building. It had a large overhang, very sloping with about 3 feet between the roofs. So with our hands extended on his grandma's house and our feet on the next-door neighbor building, there we were looking down, knowing that with one wrong move, it would all be over. I didn't say a word. I would fear heights later on in life greatly because of this incident. One of the police noticed the screen was off this closed window and put his gun out there ordering us to get inside. What a relief! I grew up hating the police but I sure was glad to see them that day. I never told God thank you then but I'm telling you now Lord, THANK YOU!

Evil was always present and working in my life because I was making bad choices. I look back and can say without a doubt my heavenly FATHER was there watching and had HIS ANGELS surrounding me or things could have been a whole lot worse. I DIDN'T CHANGE MY LIFESTYLE THOUGH. IT JUST GOT WORSE THROUGH THE YEARS.

We also found out some things about Paul later. That episode with us was not his first. He got his thrills by raping women with their boyfriend or husband present. He had done this many times using knives or guns and beating the men when they protested. A couple of years later I was listening to the radio and Paul and his brother in California were facing the electric chair for murdering an actor. It didn't surprise me. At that time I had a HARDHEART and thought, good. Now, I feel shame for thinking that and hope that he gave his life to Christ before he died.

Another close encounter with death was when my friend Marilyn, the dancer, picked me up in her boyfriend's T-Bird. We bought a gallon of Mogan David wine and had been drinking whiskey prior to that. It was about 2 AM when another car with 2 guys pulled up along side of us on Cicero Avenue. They wanted to drag race us. Cicero is a four lane city street in Chicago. When the light turned green we zoomed off. We were winning when the next light turned red with traffic. Marilyn slammed on the brakes and we did a U-Turn. We ended up front bumper to front bumper with those guys. It was a miracle no one was hurt except our vehicles. Instead of praising God we were so mad that our wine was all gone. It had spilt all over us and looked like blood. We were cursing so loudly. She knew her boyfriend was going to be upset. We didn't stop to think we could have been killed along with innocent people as well. About a year later Marilyn went to Tennessee to visit some friends. She and her friend were killed when their car hit a tree. She had been speeding and drinking. She was only 19. The devil has destroyed so many lives physically, emotionally and spiritually. Look around and you'll see the evidence of his dirty work. Through the years, so many of our street corner or bar friends have died. Overdose, accident or murder have been the main reasons. Many have ended up in jail as well. I have been arrested numerous times but never convicted or did time. That's a miracle in itself.

Carl and I were together for about a year and a half. He wouldn't work and never owned a car. He got his so-called thrills from stealing cars and joy riding. He didn't try to sell the cars or even the parts - he just drove them while he got drunk. I even drove one myself. He had parked one overnight in front of our apartment and I took it to another neighborhood. Many women are in jail because of association with a male who has influenced them for evil. Of course many men are in jail because of their bad choices with women. If I knew then what I know now about the Lord the whole course of my life could have so much happier. That's why young people have to be reached for Jesus. The exciting thing going on is that God is raising up a young generation who will make a commitment to the Lord. They are taking a stand for holiness; to live a G-RATED LIFE (GODLY) and not let peer pressure compromise their walk with the Lord. I pray this book will help not only adults but youth as well.

Well Carl sure suffered from his bad choices. One night Carl stole a car and took it across two state lines. That's a Federal offense and he did three years in a Kentucky state prison. He left for prison three days before our daughter, Patti MayJeanne, was born - pretty little Patti. How precious a gift from God she was. Although at age 19, I was so full of selfishness that I never really recognized this gift that God intends all mothers to see. The devil blinds us to our blessings and keeps us from a life that has fulfillment, peace and joy as a Christian. More self-pity set in as feelings of abandonment came during the birth of our precious daughter. I was so blessed to have a mother who also was there for me during my heartaches and trials. I have found out that the Lord is always there for us even when we think no one sees or even cares. He says in His word, ***"I'll never leave you or forsake you"***. So if you're going through something difficult right now and there's not even a human there to comfort you, JESUS IS WITH YOU.

I was devastated and heartbroken and spent many hours crying. Mom let me and Patti move in with her. Carl and I wrote each other everyday, with me promising to wait. Three years seemed to be an eternity to me. I felt like I was without hope and no future. We had a crazy relationship though and only God knows what would have become of it if we'd stayed together. We both drank heavily and both he and I had real bad tempers. We'd cuss and fight, and he'd even hit me with a belt. I previously mentioned that when I was 16 I started going to bars and shooting pool. So when I met Carl we not only hung out on street corners but went to bars where you never knew when a fight would break out. There are some wild neighborhoods in Chicago and that's what I liked and of course didn't have the sense to be afraid. Many times he'd want to go after it got late but I'd persuade him to stay for just one more game. I was really addicted to gambling on the pool table. It became a down fall in my life for many more years and relationships to come. Carl was real jealous and I realize now why. I enjoyed all the attention I got from men when I would walk in somewhere. I was a flirt. That hard heart had produced a desire for enjoying being in control. I look back now and I really can't blame men for my own wrong choices. Although I had been a victim of other men's evil choices I would make many evil choices myself and victimize others through the years.

I'm glad God is forgiving and I have forgiven myself as well. I'm no longer that hardhearted person. The night I asked JESUS to come into my heart and life, my heart became soft, loving, kind, merciful, and forgiving. There's a verse in the Bible that says, ***"I WILL GIVE YOU A NEW HEART, I WILL TAKE YOUR STONEY HEART OF SIN AND GIVE YOU A NEW HEART OF LOVE.(Ez.36:26)*** I really didn't like the attitudes and bad feelings that were deep inside of me. When a bad attitude pops up now, God helps me to get an attitude adjustment and I don't carry those bad feelings that will end up in destructive choices.

One night before Carl went to jail, we were at a party where almost everyone got homemade tattoos. They were made from India ink, needles and thread. I had Carl's initials put on my back, each letter of my name put on my right hand fingers and a dagger put on the top of my right hand. After watching him I put some on my own self. I put Carl's letters of his name, on my left fingers and a cross on my forearm. I didn't realize what a cross really stood for then. Now I do. A cross shows how much love Jesus has for each of us and offers us a new life, a fresh start. A life that can have all guilt and shame removed and be forgiven of every dirty rotten thought, action, or attitude. THANK YOU JESUS! Of course no one had shared that with me as of yet until many more years of destruction came. That's why I'm writing this book, so others can have what I have - a personal relationship with a loving forgiving God.

After Carl served his sentence and had been out for four years, his best friend would put a gun to his head and kill him over drugs. How sad a day it was! I remember his funeral. I hate the devil. He's the one behind the heartaches. I WOULD SOON GO FROM THE FRYING PAN TO THE FIRE WITH MORE DESTRUCTIVE CHOICES

CHAPTER FOUR
A CHEATING HEART
- BETRAYAL AND PROSTITUTION -

From the frying pan to the fire is an understatement. More destructive choices followed in my life. When Patti was one month old I started leaving her with my mom while I hit the bars every night. I felt abandoned and alone. So off I went looking for love in all the wrong places and faces. I met Peter in a bar. He was a part-time drummer in a band. Good looking and a smooth talker, he didn't have a regular job either. Here we go again!

Almost immediately I moved in with him, his alcoholic mom, his sister and her boyfriend. Everybody drank and life was crazy. His elderly mom would get wild and throw glass baby bottles and booze bottles, all the while cursing as loud as she could. When she was sober she was real sweet. Like most people including myself, booze makes you a different person. Most people who drink or do drugs are really nice folks. That's why I have spent years specializing in ministering to people with various addictions that THE DEVIL HAS USED AND ABUSED. It's time to expose him for the destruction that he has caused in so many countless lives. Jesus said, ***"YOU SHALL KNOW THE TRUTH AND THE TRUTH SHALL SET YOU FREE" (John 8:32).***

Mom wouldn't let me take Patti to their house and it's a good thing she didn't. I started dancing again because nobody worked in that house. I was given a business card by one of the customers at one of those clubs. He was a photographer and I was excited. I imagined fame and fortune for posing in magazines as a model. When I walked into his studio I was very impressed. It appeared just as you've seen in the movies. There were huge colorful backdrops of gorgeous scenes, cameras everywhere, and lots of bright lights. He had told me to bring a bikini and a towel, as the first scene was a beautiful ocean background with various shades of blue. It was so exciting!

Needless to say, this did not turn out to be what I'd hoped for. This was all a pretense. This man wanted to EXPLOIT AND USE ME! That's exactly what I allowed him to do. MONEY, MONEY, MONEY! The devil convinces us that we have to do certain things in life to survive what we perceive as a dog-eat-dog world. Many have even made career choices or compromises to attain money. It doesn't matter if it's selling drugs, alcohol, your body, gambling, or telling little white lies in so called respectable business jobs. I don't have to compromise my faith and morals to get my needs met. JESUS is my PROVIDER (Phil. 4: 19). He makes opportunities arise to meet my needs - nothing is coincidence or luck. The next time you get in a jam, ask God to help you. Don't try to do it your way and you'll be amazed how he'll come through for you. Many times it seems as if God comes through at the last minute. He does this to strengthen and test our faith. Your faith will grow and your love for Him will grow as you see this UNSEEN God meet your need. It's awesome!

When this so called modeling session was over, I felt degraded. I have no idea what nasty magazines those photos went to. I'm sure he was making tall dollars USING ME. All I know is that at the time I was thrilled with what I thought was a wad of money. That became one of many sessions that would follow through the years, just like dancing, when I needed quick money.

I sure had a lot of heartaches from the two and a half years I lived with Peter. He thought he was God's gift to women. God made man to be with only one woman. There is a great need in all of us that wants to BE DESIRED. Actually God gave us that need and when in a godly union between a man and a woman that need can be met. When we are not born again and yielding to The Holy Spirit guiding us, this need can really go berserk. Even Christians have to be alert to the evil spirits of WANTING TO BE DESIRED, FOUND ATTRACTIVE, WANTING OTHERS TO NOTICE OUR VALUE AND TALENTS, ETC. We need to see that these needs can only be met by God. He values us, desires a relationship with us, and has given us talents to be used by Him. Many people have cheated on someone else because of these evil obsessions. That type of destructive choice not only ends up destroying ourselves but devastating so many others. It usually starts out seemingly innocent with the opposite sex giving words of flattery and admiration. Read chapters 6 & 7 in the Book of Proverbs. It's warning a man about a smooth talking woman, but it also serves as a warning to ladies. I've been on both ends of that spectrum. I'VE BEEN CHEATED ON, AND I'VE BEEN THE CHEATER. Along with flattery comes empathy for what you're going through (such as the wife or girlfriend not meeting your needs or their faults). Then they want to console you with a hug. Sometimes it all starts with joking around, teasing, trying to get the other in a good mood. BEWARE if you see these signs, don't spend time alone with the opposite sex or the Spirit of Lust will raise its ugly head. It's devastating not only for you but your precious loved one that God gave you. When God said to not fornicate (have sex outside of marriage) or commit adultery (have sex with someone other than your spouse) it wasn't to be mean. It was for our own good. Such heartache can be spared when we follow God's way.

  The SPIRIT OF LUST comes at first as a thought. It can come through someone showing unusual interest in you, or by what you've seen in a magazine, internet site, or other type of media, or even through what music you listen to. That's why it's very important that you monitor what you're feeding your mind and heart. The devil will make sure he gives you an OPPORTUNITY to put those THOUGHTS into ACTION. As I look back, that is what happened to me. When I opened the door for sin, it came bursting in, putting me as its slave. At first, it brought pleasure and excitement, but it quickly led to low self esteem, guilt and shame. When illicit sex happens, you eventually end up FEELING USED and that you USED OTHERS.

  At that time in my life I didn't know what I know now: that LIFE IS A SPIRITUAL BATTLE, and we need GOD'S SPIRIT WITHIN US to be able to SAY NO. The world is looking for love in all the wrong places and faces. IT'S ONLY

FOUND IN GOD. GOD IS LOVE and He first loved us when we were yet sinners.

Five months after meeting Peter I became pregnant with my second child, Bobby Daniel. A big blue eyed precious baby boy. Again I didn't realize as I do now what a wonderful gift children are. The Bible says, **"God formed all of us when we're yet in our mother's womb" (Psalm 139)**. None of us are accidents. We all have a divine purpose and plan. We were created for GOD'S pleasure (Rev. 4:11). God gave us children to enjoy and many of us before being saved have felt that they were more of a burden. Some of us have looked for fulfillment in people, places and careers. I did at that time, not knowing what I know now.

I was truly blinded to the beautiful blessings God gave me. I always loved my children but through the years they spent lots of time in the care of babysitters and family. How sad! The pursuit of happiness is not found in those things. Fulfillment comes from having a pure personal relationship with God and the family He gives you. When The Lord is put first in your life, peace and contentment follow. Appreciation for the family that He gives brings a heart of gratitude and thankfulness.

During my pregnancy, I suspected Peter was cheating on me. My BEST FRIEND and him would tease and laugh with each other excessively. Also Peter would go out in the evening and come back all hours of the night. He didn't have a regular job so he had to be up to something.

One of his best friends told me he was sleeping with MY BEST FRIEND. I would get in my car with my bottle of booze and ride around Chicago trying to catch them. That's a sickening feeling in the pit of your stomach. Any of you who have gone through the CHEATING GAME know what it's like.

One evening I saw them in a car and drove so crazy trying to run them over. I ran into their bumper several times but they escaped due to traffic. I got hired as a cab driver and used to drive all over Chicago looking for them in it. One night I got so drunk and kept the cab overnight and lost my job. I was also filled with the spirits of JEALOUSY and HATRED. This happened during my pregnancy, so when my precious baby was born and was three weeks old, I headed out for MY BEST FRIEND'S house.

A big party was going on. I had hitch hiked a ride with a stranger and got dropped off there. I went to her back door and demanded she come out. I told her that I was going to whip her. She came out along with everyone at the party. I was alone but fearless. I was so full of HATE and wanted REVENGE. There was about a foot of snow on the ground, as it was early February. I punched her and down we went in the snow, putting her in a headlock. The neighbors called the police and when we heard sirens everyone starting yanking us apart and ran into the house. The only part I can laugh about is that unbeknownst to them, I ran inside too and hid in her closet. I could hear the police asking everyone questions about me. Then I heard snickering and one of Peter's friends was in the closet too. There was a warrant for his arrest and he was hiding too.

After the police left, I came out and everyone freaked out because I had been there all along. I remember feeling so empty and numb. REVENGE had not made me feel any better. Even if I had killed her I realized getting even doesn't make you feel better not one little bit. Peter had left when I first showed up and of course somehow I let him smooth talk me again. He continued to CHEAT ON ME with not only her, but others. I continued to drink and throw temper tantrums. Throwing baby food jars and other glass items at him was a common occurrence. I'd cuss him something terrible and we'd fight like cats and dogs. One night while he slept I started burning his black leather motorcycle jacket in our living room. He woke up, put out the fire, and another fight was on. He was a little afraid of me because I always threatened him with a butcher knife that I'd get him while he slept. I had a very bad temper and JEALOUSY AND REVENGE were part of my character that was induced by alcohol. What wasted years of my precious young life! This was insanity. This type of lifestyle is not unusual in our world. The same devil has been at work for thousands of years destroying people's lives.

During this time period I resorted to dancing again to make quick money as Peter didn't work. It was through these nightclubs that I would meet wealthy business men that would become my "sugar daddies". PROSTITUTION! They offered big, big money - even more than I got paid for dancing. They would get a room in big fancy hotels with champagne and food. They all drove Cadillac's or Lincolns and I would be so impressed, at least in the beginning). I'd tell myself, "Peter's CHEATING on me, so why not?" A HARD HEART was needed and an attitude of, "if YOU'RE trying to USE ME, I'M GOING TO USE YOU AS WELL".

I hate to admit it, but these three temptations: DANCING, MODELING, AND SUGAR DADDIES, would be part of my life off and on until age 35 when I was saved. SO, I BECAME A CHEATER AS WELL.

Three months after my sweet baby boy was born I became pregnant with my third child, Peggy Sue. Now Peter happened to be at home when Bobby was born because it was in the afternoon. When Peggy Sue was born it was 5:30 AM and he was out and about as usual. My precious mom and wonderful step dad were there for me as usual. I thank God for their love and faithfulness to me. The Lord was there, too, I just didn't know it.

I reasoned that surely two babies would want to make Peter change. He was so proud of them and I know he loved them but there was a spiritual battle raging within him as there was in me.

Peggy Sue was another precious baby girl that was only 364 days younger than her brother, Bobby Daniel. Patti MayJeanne was only two years and three months old when Peggy Sue was born.

THE AMERICAN DREAM LIFE was about to happen for me and my children. Without God as priority in our lives though, the HOME WRECKERS would come and DESTROY us all.

CHAPTER FIVE
HOME WRECKERS
- ALCOHOL, DOMESTIC VIOLENCE, ADULTERY, PORNOGRAPHY AND GAMBLING -

When Peggy Sue was about three weeks old I would discover a whole new life. At this point in my life, I was 21 years old, had a cheating, unemployed boyfriend, with ongoing domestic violence mixed with alcoholism. I was broke, with no one to love and care for the four of us.

One day there came a knock on the door and there stood a nice looking young man looking for Peter. He was clean cut and had recently come home from Vietnam. I invited him in and offered him a beer. He showed great interest in the kids as he held and played with them. I was overjoyed to see someone be so attentive to the kids because Peter was hardly ever at home. I'd wash and iron his clothes, tell him how nice he looked, and off he'd go into the arms of someone else. Although it was a sad situation, when you're in love you'll put up with a lot of heartache. Unless you've been in a similar situation, it's hard to comprehend the craziness of it all.

There were many times in my life that I've wondered how someone could do or put up with all that they did. I'D SAY, "I'D NEVER DO THAT", or "I'D NEVER PUT UP WITH THAT". Then later in life I'd find myself doing something similar or worse. The Bible says not to judge others, but to pray for them.

Even now with my life so completely changed and turned around, I have to remember what I used to be like before Jesus came into my heart and life. None of us are above anyone else. As a Christian, we know Jesus makes the difference, and He's the answer for all of life's problems. It's a SPIRITUAL BATTLE and once you know the truth and act on that truth by committing to follow the Lord, He empowers you to be able to make good choices. We have to look past people's choices to sin and see their heart as He sees it. I'm glad Jesus loved me enough to knock on my heart and ask me to let Him in (Revelation 3:20). I'm so glad that I didn't refuse his voice of love, and shut Him out anymore.

Roy kept coming to the apartment and asking for Peter. Soon I realized he had a great interest in me and I loved the attention. He was a gentleman, not pushy, and very kind. He wasn't like all the other street people or bar people I had met. I was infatuated by the fact that he brought food and beer with him. He had a job. A real job!! He was a tradesman, a pipe fitter in the union. He drove a new car and had no children or had ever been married. He had just turned 21. This was all too good to be true for me.

When Peter found out about Roy he wanted to kill us. The cheater was mad he was getting cheated on. We heard he had a gun, so I quickly packed up what belongings I owned and moved in with Roy. He took in me and my three babies.

Shortly afterwards, Peter married my best friend, which I felt was purely a payback. I heard later that he kept cheating on her and would beat her worse than me. At that time in my life I loved juicy news and laughed and said, "She wanted what I had and she got it, even worse". The spirit of hate was still oppressing me.

I couldn't believe the wonderful change Roy brought into my life. He even told me he didn't want me to go-go dance anymore. He had a good job and I could stay at home while he took care of us. WOW! This was a first. He genuinely loved and cared for me and the kids. Crying and diapers didn't faze him a bit. I stayed in love with Peter for quite some time, but as each day passed, my love grew stronger for Roy.

As a Christian now, I can see the similarities of marriage with our relationship with the Lord. When you first make a commitment to God (to love honor and obey) generally a great love is not felt. Then as you begin to learn the character of God and notice His acts of kindness in your life, you can't help but fall in love with Him. It is a love that grows with each passing day.

That's what happened to me with Roy. As he showed his love by continual acts of kindness, I realized finally what a wonderful man I had. Roy asked me to marry him after we had lived together for about a year. I wore a white dress, had a nice set of wedding rings and was married in a little church. Something was wrong right from the start though. We weren't aware of the reason why, as most people aren't. The missing ingredient was that God was only mentioned by name. He was not invited into our individual hearts or our marriage. He was not placed first, so as time would go on Satan would bring havoc to this happy home. He loves being A HOME WRECKER!!

Remember, we're in a SPIRITUAL BATTLE! When the enemy sees two people united, he's out to destroy that unity. Look around at the divorce rate - even with Christians. After you're saved you have to maintain your commitment and never let up. To maintain your commitment to Christ requires discipline. Going to church, reading your Bible, sharing your faith, and praying are needed for not only your personal strength, but for keeping your marriage strong as well. Later on I'll share with you how I did let up and the bad consequences that followed.

As I look back now I asked God what went wrong? How did this dream marriage fall apart? It didn't happen overnight. Most of the time when life gets out of control it's because one or both couples have given control over to the enemy. It's a spiritual battle (Ephesians 6:12) and there are EVIL SPIRITS at work to destroy you. The devil is a HOME WRECKER! He offers us many temptations and if we choose them we suffer the destructive consequences. He WRECKS not only our HOMES but our lives, our spouses, children, family members and all others who our lives influence and touch.

Roy and I both came into this marriage as drinkers. I for one definitely let this temptation take me way past being an occasional drinker to being an out of control, unmanageable, ALCOHOLIC. Unfortunately, I wouldn't admit this until years after our HOME WAS WRECKED. ALCOHOLISM IS A HOME WRECKER. For those of you who have "been there, done that", you know the devastation it brings to all those in your life.

I never realized that I had a problem, as I viewed myself as a social drinker. As a teenager, I bowed to peer pressure. Then later I played the blame game from the incest in my past. I would always MINIMIZE my drinking. I would tell myself, "you don't drink every day, all day, morning, noon and night like those you'd see lying in the streets at night". I felt drinking on weekends with my husband was just having a good time. I was in deeper though because when he was tired and wanted to go home, I didn't - especially if there was a pool table there. GAMBLING was another evil spirit for HOME WRECKING. We'd fight like cats and dogs over my DRINKING and GAMBLING. I wasn't ready to quit!

I also RATIONALIZED why I drank. PROBLEMS, BILLS, KIDS, STRESS, ETC. I had a million excuses. Who doesn't? Whether it's alcohol or drugs, the bottom line is that there doesn't have to be an excuse. It's our choice and when Jesus reveals Himself to us, it's up to us to choose Him. When we do, He gives us THE POWER TO KEEP THAT CHOICE.

I had a likeable personality when I wasn't drinking and could even be sweet (at times). When drinking though, I put on beer and shot "muscles". I thought I was tough and all irritations that had built up would just explode. No wonder I ended up in harm's way so many times. I had a potty mouth that spilled out four letter words even in normal conversation - I didn't have to be angry. I was petite but proudly boasted, "dynamite comes in small packages." I'd get right up in Roy's face and dare him to hit me, all the while cursing fiercely. He'd push me to get me out of his face and I'd push back. Before you knew it, we'd be out of control. The four kids would wake up to hear and see this ugly scene. How horrible for them.

Needless to say, I became a thorn in my husband's side under these EVIL INFLUENCES. No wonder they call drinking or drugging, "UNDER THE INFLUENCE". It is an EVIL Spirit. Thanks be to God, I'm under another kind of influence now - a GODLY INFLUENCE - THE HOLY SPIRIT. You see, Jesus died to break Satan's power and influence over our lives. He came to set us free so that we be all that He created us to be.

There is POWER IN THE BLOOD that He shed at Calvary! I'm living proof to this day! All we have to do is

1. Confess that we are a sinner and can't change ourselves.
2. Believe that only Jesus can change you and ask Him to save you
3. Make a CHOICE to live for GOD with all of your heart and TURN AWAY from all of your OLD ways.

Be willing to give Him your X-RATED sins (no matter how big or small. ALL have sinned in some ways. He'll then give you a NEW life (2 Cor. 5:17) and you too can live a G-RATED (GODLY) LIFESTYLE, LIKE ME. As you read on, you'll see I didn't receive this truth until more wasted years passed. That's why I'm so compelled to write this book.

Beneath the outward appearance of your life, is a wonderful human being God created. You are precious and valuable to Him. My story needs to be told, so others can be spared some of the heartaches and destruction I've experienced. The grass always looks greener on the other side. The devil always gives it that appearance but it is actually burnt up when you get there.

The Old Testament is full of actual accounts of Godly men and women who sinned. When they repented (made a U-Turn), God used their lives. Those true stories are there for us to learn from their example so, WE DON'T GO THERE! That is one of the reasons I'm writing this book. ALL THAT GLITTERS ISN'T GOLD – sometimes IT'S FOOL'S GOLD. It is simply IMITATION compared to the life God wants to give you if you'll live for Him.

Soon after Roy and I were married we had a four bedroom, full basement raised ranch house built. I couldn't believe that this was happening to me. ME! We moved from Chicago to the suburbs, fifty miles north, to a better environment for the kids to be raised. I was used to dumpy apartments and some even with cockroaches so thick you'd wake up with them on you. I ate more than my share of pinto beans, macaroni and cheese, and peanut butter. I was now blessed with a life that was a far cry from what it used to be.

A BRAND NEW HOME! Wow! I even got to pick out the colors for the carpet, paint, tile, etc. What an experience! It's a shame THE HOME WRECKER would end up destroying this happy home. Now we can't put the blame on the devil even though he's the spiritual influence behind the destruction. God gave us a free will to make choices. I'm merely pointing out the spiritual battle that occurs when we're confronted with choices. The songwriter said it well, "I once was blind but now I see". The devil blinds our eyes to the truth until Jesus sends us the good news through a messenger. I'm one of his many messengers and you can be too, if you're not already. Because I was so spiritually blinded at the time, I WOULD CONTINUALLY WRECK OUR HOME with all of these vices. I have finally taken personal responsibility for my own choices and quit blaming everything and everybody. Yes, I was influenced by evil but NOW I know the truth. The truth has set ME FREE! Free to make Godly choices.

I soon became pregnant with my fourth child, precious little Dorothie Ruth (Dee). This would be Roy's only child. He was such a good daddy to all the kids and showed no partiality. Roy would adopt the other three. He wanted them all to have his last name and feel more like family. There's not many men who will do this type of act of love.

GAMBLING was another HOME WRECKER! I shared with you earlier how shooting pool for money or booze became a destructive obsession for me. Everybody likes to win. When we play a game, whether it's sports, cards, board game etc., we like the idea of winning. That in itself is not wrong as long as it's balanced and you learn to not be angry or depressed when you lose, but playing for money can get way out of hand. Addiction to gambling or any other destructive habit can bring about HOME AND PERSONAL LIFE WRECKAGE!

There is a driving force, an obsession that compels a person to keep indulging. GAMBLING would take on other forms besides the POOL TABLE. Bingo, poker, horse races, etc.

No one purposely sets out to become addicted to anything. Give the devil an inch and he'll take a mile. My girlfriend, Ruth, told me, "Kandi, when you lived for the devil you lived for him good, when you live for God, you live for Him good."

I had a best friend from Chicago who moved to the suburbs too. Her name is Dorothy, who I named my youngest daughter after. She is married with two sons, who at that time were about the same age as my children. She had not lived near as crazy a life as I had but made some bad choices as a teenager. Then God put a good hardworking man in her life. They were married and he bought her a brand new home as well.

We lived close to each other and soon we were coffee-clutching with lots of neighbors. I'd have up as many as twelve ladies over almost every day. The reason that most of them came to my house was that I had the most children. I had four children in four and a half years time. When the youngest, Dee, was born, the oldest Patti was not even in kindergarten until five months later. Barefoot and pregnant! Life seemed so normal for awhile. I'd watch soap operas and become discontent with my seemingly boring life. I know now what you watch, read or listen to will affect your choices.

I met wonderful friends and neighbors who even though they were UNLIKE me and my past, they accepted and loved me. We'd play poker during the day starting out with penny ante and going to dollar ante. I'd cut corners on my groceries so that I could have more money to gamble with even though Roy would give me money. It became expensive to play. I started going to Bingo one night a week and eventually played 4 - 5 times a week. It was very costly. Roy made good money. He made more than some of our neighbors. Because of my gambling habit though, credit cards, and debt got OUT OF CONTROL. We were constantly fighting because there was never enough money to pay all those bills we'd acquired. The big paycheck became not big enough. DEBT IS A HOMEWRECKER caused by one or both person's appetite for more material things. It's not worth your marriage to try to obtain things. Things are not what's valuable - it's your family!

My friends and neighbors didn't get out of hand like I did. I was the only one drinking during the day while we played cards. I was the only one drinking during Bingo. I was the wild one of the bunch. They would all laugh at me and make fun of me. I was the so-called life of the party. I'd tell the nastiest jokes and be swearing all the time. When a person really gets saved there's a definite change.

Roy and I would throw booze parties. We had a bar and pool table in our basement. Lots of couples would come. Not everyone would get as nuts as me. After a few drinks they would go home. Me, I drank on, and on, and on. Many times I'd plead for Roy to get a babysitter so we could go to the bar and shoot pool, and of course gamble. Roy and I had many fights at the bar because I didn't want to leave. I was obsessed! I CRAVED the GAME as much as the ALCOHOL.

I loved my children and thought I was being a good mom. Even though I'd play kid board games with them, go the beach, go on outings, and school field trips, I fell short in many areas. It's so sad that I can't turn back the clock and be the G-RATED (GODLY) mom that they so desperately needed.

I cussed my kids when they didn't behave. Then I'd spank them when they cussed. I never actually beat them physically, but emotionally can be just as damaging. I used babysitters a lot so I could selfishly go have a good time. I thought because I never left them alone that I was a good mom. I drank in front of them and later when they were in their teens I smoked pot with them. They heard my screams and cursing as Roy and I fought all hours of the night, waking them up. How sad!

I have tears in my eyes remembering their sweet little faces who loved their mommy. All they wanted out of life is what everybody wanted - to not only have someone say they love them but to spend quality time with them. But no, I was TOO SELFISH!

Yes, I know I can't turn back the clock. God has showed me that it's better late than never to make a U-TURN. I've asked their forgiveness and of course God's. He entrusted me with their precious lives. I may not have been a GODLY example then but I'm living my life trying to be more like JESUS now. I'm not perfect, but willing. I've learned to forgive myself.

I encourage any of you who are where I used to be to remember: GOD ALLOWS U-TURNS. If you're carrying guilt, give it to the Lord. We can't live in the past, but with God in our life He can and does restore relationships. He will heal your broken heart and your family's as well. It does take time. Wait on God and he'll heal the hurt.

When the kids were 3,5,6,and 7, a young pastor knocked on our door. He asked if he could pick up my kids on Sunday morning for church. At that time I had no family members or not even one friend who was born again. I guess you could say I was agnostic. I thought this would be great for the wrong reason. I always went to the bar on Saturday nights and would have a terrible hangover on Sunday. So, I thought that after I got them on the bus, I could go back to sleep. Even though my motive was selfish, this event would start turning the table on the devil. Total victory didn't come right away, but through the years of seed planting and watering, a harvest of souls would follow. THANK YOU PASTOR!

Sunday school teachers and bus drivers, youth workers of all ages, you are important! You can MAKE A DIFFERENCE! My four children were the first to be saved in our family. More people would follow through the years. God heard these precious intercessory prayers of my children as they interceded for their family to be saved as well. Of course with no Godly life style at home to be an example of a true Christian, their choices would also be influenced by the evil one. Parents, once we know the truth, it's time to take a stand for Christ and LIVE THE LIFE OF A TRUE CHRISTIAN BEFORE THEM. They need an example. Even if they are adults now, it's not too late to make a U-TURN.

Years later when I got saved, I reminded my children that my salvation along with the salvation of their grandparents were because of their intercessory prayers. His timing is different than ours but none the less, it happened. Now, I pray for some of them to return wholeheartedly to the Lord. I have seen miracles already happening. Acts 16:31 is God's promise, if we'd believe, OUR WHOLE HOUSEHOLD WILL BE SAVED.

When the kids were real young my friends Ruth, Dorothy and I did housecleaning jobs. We made our own hours and the pay rate was real good. When I got home I was so wore out that I didn't feel like cleaning my own. Even though I had a brand new home and new furniture, I grew discontent as I compared it to those other fancy homes. I should have had a thankful heart and remembered where I had been prior to meeting Roy. Instead, I always wanted more material things, so that I could keep up with the neighbors. As I watched the soap operas, I grew discontent and restless for excitement, not happy being "tied down". DISCONTENT is a HOME WRECKER!

I began bowling on a daytime women's league. I had a lot of fun with my two friends Lily and Terry. Terry and I probably were the only ones who drank during those early morning hours. I was foul mouthed and dirty joking. A few years later Lily became Born Again and would end up being instrumental in my spiritual birth.

When Lily got saved she quit bowling but would stop by once in a while to witness to me. I'd be sitting there with my shot and beer listening politely. I remember laughing and saying, "Yeah, maybe one of these days when I get old, God might use me in prostitute's and stripper's lives." I prophesied to my own self and didn't even realize it.

As time would pass Lily found herself in deep intercessory prayer for me. God would bring me to her mind and she'd weep and cry deeply for my soul. Every now and then she'd invite me to church even though she was a timid person. God had not only my mom and step-dad praying for me, but he was raising up an army of prayer warriors. They were BOMBARDING THE SPIRITUAL REALM on my behalf, for the spiritual battle that was going on for my soul. KEEP PRAYING FAMILY MEMBERS FOR YOUR FAMILY, FRIENDS AND THIS LOST WORLD. Later I'll share how this battle became VICTORIOUS.

About this time I also met my best friend Katy, her husband Will, and their four children who were about my children's age. Katy and I had something in common, we both loved pool. She had a pool table in her basement, too. Oh Boy! She was the only woman I had ever met who was better than me. Not only better, but she became the top woman shooter in our county. We joined a women's pool league that shot once a week. Three games each, with four women on a team, opposing four other women, from a different team. Of course we shot in bars that would sponsor these four women teams. We'd then travel within our county, to a different bar each week, challenging each other. Score was kept like bowling. At the end of the season you'd win money and trophies. Wow, did I love that!

I'd get soused. Then I wouldn't go home when it was over around 10 or so. I wanted to keep DRINKING and SHOOTING POOL. Katy would go home to her husband and kids, but not me. A driving force inside of me kept me out until the bars closed.

This took a heavy toll on my marriage. My poor husband was getting sick of this. Eventually these destructive choices led to ADULTERY. I'd end up so drunk and be like a helpless little baby not even able to walk or drive. So at closing time at the bars I'd find myself with perfect strangers taking advantage of me. BEING USED!

At that point I was mentally and physically beyond the capability of choosing to do what is right. ALCOHOL will impair you so bad that you'll do things you thought you'd never do. It's the best choice to just not to take that first drink or drug. It will TAKE YOU FARTHER THAN YOU WANT TO GO, and KEEP YOU LONGER THAN YOU WANT TO STAY.

When that first encounter of ADULTERY happened I felt so much shame and guilt. I also remember praying God, don't let me be pregnant or have a disease. It's a miracle I didn't. Before we give our lives to God we ask Him for help with BIG problems. They call them foxhole prayers.

I couldn't tell anyone about this, especially my husband. Dark secrets will eat you up inside. That's one of the benefits of being saved. You can dump all your dirty laundry out to him and he cleans you up and forgives you. Repentance is needed though. Repentance is turning from your actions and being committed to not doing it again. If you truly mean it, God knows - you can't fool Him. He will give you the power to OVERCOME.

I tried to rationalize my behavior by blaming everything and everybody. It was a pity party, poor me mentality. If you play with fire you will get burnt. Some bad consequences happened during some of these evenings. I was robbed once, raped again, got into fights with women, almost went to jail with five driving tickets one night, wet my pants and had diarrhea, and vomiting. Alcoholism is not a pretty sight or fun and exciting. Commercials make it look like everyone is having so much fun. You can't even remember if you had a good time or not. Taking that first drink may have you off to the races coming in last. DON'T GO THERE! Through time I tuned out my conscience (and the voice of God) and it would ultimately WRECK MY HOME!

Roy and I would fight like crazy and we even separated for a while. Then I'd mellow out and not drink for weeks or even months. I didn't really believe I had an alcohol problem.

For a little while it appeared my life was normal. I got my G.E.D. diploma just by going to the college three days taking the tests. I never took G.E.D. preparation classes and had been out of school 12 years. I was so proud. Then I went to real estate school. Roy went with me to Springfield, Illinois to take the test. I got my license and began to sell. I loved real estate. It was so rewarding helping people find their dream home. I also felt respectable. It gave me self esteem.

After a year and a half of many nights of drinking followed by next morning hangovers, I lost my job. I didn't pursue this career again until a few years later, and then only for a short time.

However, I did learn about advertising, promoting, time management, sales and other business skills by going to real estate seminars. These training skills would be used years later by the devil to promote a very evil business, "KANDI ROSE PRODUCTIONS", my own Strip-O-Gram and Theatrical

Booking Agency. Later these same skills would promote THE GOOD NEWS, this book and my own Christian Publishing Company. GOD IS GOOD!!!

During my marriage with Roy a spirit of LUST developed into an obsession for PORNOGRAPHY. I started out reading bedtime romance novels. Novels with just tidbits of fornication and adultery threaded throughout the books. I'd rate them as PG-13. Then I changed to books that had strong sexual language in them. I'd rate them as R-RATED. Then I would get books that would get graphic not only with language but very detailed and explicit. I'd rate them as X-RATED.

I began feeding this appetite of lust with not only what I could READ but now I wanted what I could SEE. So I bought X-RATED Raw PORNOGRAPHY and of course hid them from my husband and children. Later in life, I visited ADULT BOOK STORES and saw the peep shows. Later I added AN ADULT X-RATED MOVIE CHANNEL to my cable TV package. If computers had been popular then, I'm positive that I would have been hooked to internet porn. PRAISE GOD, I'M FREE TODAY BY THE BLOOD OF JESUS!

You don't even need to mess with seeing underwear commercials on T.V. Turn the channel right away. Your mind is like a computer with a memory system. Scenes will stay in your mind, sometimes for years. Of course when you get saved, God can cleanse your mind by reading His Word. He can renew and transform your mind (Romans 12). Constantly guard your eyes, ears, and mind. This is a powerful evil that can't be stopped by your own will power. There is GOOD NEWS: When JESUS died on the cross and said, "IT IS FINISHED", He broke the devil's power of sin over us! When you accept Him and make a wholehearted commitment to live for Him, YOU TOO CAN BE FREE. Sins and habits of every kind, no matter how big or small can be gone through making JESUS your personal Savior.

Of course a few years later I not only viewed PORNOGRAPHY but I BECAME LIVE PORNOGRAPHY. As a Christian now, I think HOW SAD! I used to be so proud and boastful and now the only reason I tell this on myself is so that

OTHERS CAN BE SET FREE. I boast now in GOD, and give Him the credit, I DIDN'T CHANGE MYSELF. I couldn't. I tried many times to quit doing so many habits but it would only go so long before I'd be right back and even worse than before.

When you have freedom to do whatever you want, with no authority from God or any other human, will lead to destruction. Children, teenagers, married people, and even church people who desire to make their own decisions with no accountability are headed for trouble. People don't like to be accountable for their actions. "DON'T TELL ME WHAT TO DO, I'LL DO WHAT I WANT." Some who say they are Christians, don't want to quit certain things, even though they know it's wrong. No one likes correction, even by GOD. When there is no accountability, it is a breeding ground for REBELLION. That type of "FREEDOM" LEADS TO THE SLAVERY OF SIN

I thought when I got divorced it would be great not answering to anybody. How sad! I'm glad now to be accountable to God and the husband I now have.

Jesus is referred to as THE GOOD SHEPHERD and people as SHEEP. That's why I used to dress and minister to adults as "LIL BO PEEP". My new character is "SHEPHERD'S ROSE" dressed western style, carrying a stuffed sheep, portraying SHEEP ROUND-UP. When sheep are left alone with no one to watch over them, they fall prey to all kinds of danger and predators. We need a SHEPHERD to guide and direct our lives. My GOOD SHEPHERD was there all the time, but by not letting Him be in control, an EVIL SPIRITUAL REALM was in control. An EVIL SHEPHERD was guiding and directing.

My life was getting OUT OF CONTROL. So during one of those reconciliation times, Roy and I sold our house in the suburbs of Chicago and moved to Indiana. This was three hours away and in the boonies. We bought a three bedroom house in a tiny subdivision that was in the middle of nowhere. The closest small town was about a half hour's drive. When the snow came it was piled sky high. We were only there about a year. I felt so isolated and Roy worked twelve hours or more a day. We thought if I got away from my environment, like the bars, our marriage would work. But I learned that you can't run from self. The spiritual battle for your soul goes with you. Even though evil is present, I'm so glad the Lord goes with us. He and His Angels have been with us all our lives. I was never aware of HIS PRESENCE. That's why I'm writing this book so you'll know, and I pray let JESUS give you a new victorious life, and not let YOUR HOME BE WRECKED. He'll enable you to resist the evil and temptation. You'll be able to SAY "NO" TO SIN and help you make G-RATED (GODLY) choices.

Because I hadn't let JESUS be MY GOOD SHEPHERD at that time, WORSE EVIL FOLLOWED. Since the kids had been going to church in Illinois I noticed a little church not far from our house in Indiana. So one Sunday morning we all went, which was a first for us as a family. When the altar call was given, I ran to the front and so did Roy, and we said the sinner's prayer. I wanted to get rid of the guilt of adultery and make our marriage work. After the service the Pastor asked if we wanted to be baptized as a family. So we were, not really understanding what we were doing, even though he tried explaining beforehand.

As I look back now having a REAL BORN AGAIN EXPERIENCE, I asked God why I wasn't truly born again then. He told me my motives had not been right then and I had not made a whole heart commitment to follow Him. He had knocked on my heart but I had never swung open the door. The Bible says there's a difference of being sad about what you did, and the kind of Godly sorrow that leads to REPENTANCE. God knows your thoughts and motives and if you really WANT HIM. So The Holy Spirit could not come in against my will. So no change happened. Since the power of God did not indwell me, I became even worse.

Many people in church go through the motions but there's no life changing power from God like being truly born again. When The Holy Spirit actually comes into you, THERE IS A DIFFERENCE! The OLD LIFE passes away, ALL BECOMES NEW (2 Cor 5:17). You not only don't want to sin, but you think differently. You see the evil for what it is and you don't want to even be around it, much less do it. When you truly have a personal encounter with the LIVING JESUS, you only want to please Him. His love, forgiveness, and mercy give you such a gratitude for being rescued from your sins.

Since I didn't have a real born again experience, I quit church. It was the worst thing I could have done. I never gave God another chance. ***"Faith comes by hearing, and hearing by the word of God."*** So if you have not been Born Again yet, keep going. Everybody needs church. Through the worship, preaching and prayer you can learn what a great God we have and then you will someday be able to trust your life to him. He's A GOOD SHEPHERD that really loves you!

Since I made NO ACTUAL COMMITMENT (which is what I really needed) I BECAME WORSE AND WORSE. My cursing became more intense. I tried to lay the cigarettes down but ended up smoking more, up to two packs a day.

Roy worked long hours at the power plant making good money. I became bored and lonely. I was about 28. I didn't appreciate his hard work and all the nice things he provided for us. I was selfish and thought about myself. I was looking for something to fill that void in my life. I didn't understand that peace and contentment comes from a personal relationship with Jesus.

I ended up meeting an older woman who had an 18 year old son. They would come over to my house and we'd play cards while Roy was at work. It is not easy to tell these kinds of shameful sins to the world through this book. I'm only doing this so someone else may be spared grief to themselves and others - so people can know the truth about Jesus and the spiritual battle for your soul.

I hate to say it but I slept with this young guy. I felt so guilty I couldn't look Roy in the eye when he'd come home. So one day soon after, I packed all our clothes, took the four kids, and this 18 year old, and headed for Illinois. How crazy! This guy didn't even work. I left a good man who loved me for LUST. My ego was puffed up because I was having someone pay attention to me, desiring me. PROVERBS 5 - 7 instructs us to BEWARE if someone other than our spouse is paying too much attention to us at work, home, or even at church. The devil makes it seem harmless. The casual talk or "innocent" joking leads to a relationship that can lead you down the devil's path. Usually it starts out just by being friendly, then small talk, and soon a spirit of DISCONTENT for your life sets in. It always follows the same path - a spirit of LUST will come.

That relationship didn't last long. I sent him packing to his mama within a short time. Eventually Roy sold the house and came back to Illinois. I couldn't believe it. He took me back once more. You know God is like that. Even though we fail Him, he waits for us to return. Roy is a human though and adultery is a hurtful thing. He never trusted me and always accused me of cheating, so we fought and fought and fought. I saw bitterness overtake this once loving man. I understand, though, because I put him through a lot. He's married to a good woman now as I am married to a good man as well. I am truly sorry for making his life so miserable. What goes around comes around and I ended up later with a relationship that would tear my heart out. The Bible says you reap what you sow. Later, I would experience great heartache.

We can't turn back the clock but we can ask God to restore all the people we have hurt in our past. We can make amends and we also have to forgive ourselves, as God has. Romans 8:1 says, **"There is now no condemnation to those that are in Christ Jesus."**

We can choose now by the power of THE HOLY SPIRIT to make G-RATED (GODLY) decisions that will not hurt others or ourselves. Life as a true Christian is no longer living selfishly but thinking of others feelings. It is "loving our neighbors as ourselves". It is NOT USING OTHERS and NOT BEING HARDHEARTED.

By this point, all six of us are having terrible lives. With a home filled with bitterness and fighting, the innocent children were caught in the middle. They loved us both so much and hated to see us verbally and physically fight. They feared for my safety even though I'd start it most of the time. Eventually I feared for my life, as we GOT OUT OF CONTROL. It was to the point that I thought I'd end up dead. So we went to my mom and step dad's who at this time were recently born again.

They were my refuge of safety and sanity many times throughout the years - always loving me, never giving up on me, no matter how I acted or lived. They showed me God's unconditional love. They loved me when I was unlovable just like God does. That's who Jesus died for - sinners. We all have sinned in some form or another (we're born with a sinful nature) and all of us need JESUS!

I filed for DIVORCE. That was a real sad time. Deep down I really loved Roy. Divorce is as bad as death. You have so many broken dreams, disappointments, loneliness, etc. When two become one and you divorce, it's like losing a part of your body. Something's missing. The devil laughs everyday as court rooms are full of lives he's destroyed. He's a HOME WRECKER!

Yes, people have a free will to choose but he's the influence behind the scenes. That's why if the world really knew this and they would choose to live for God, life would be so different and happy. John 10:10 says that the *"enemy has come to steal, kill, and destroy but that Jesus has come to give us life and life more abundantly"*

If you have had a divorce, don't live in guilt. God knows what you've been through. What is important is that you determine NOW to live for HIM. Let Him be your comforter and heal your broken heart. Don't live in the past. Jeremiah 29:11 says, *"I know my thoughts for you are good and not evil to give you a good future."*

Something bad was about to happen for ALL OF THESE WRONG CHOICES, to all of us. I'm saddened as I recall what happened in my children's lives. They suffered emotionally - my sweet, sweet children. Their young years are gone now and I wasn't there for them. My eyes are full of tears as I'm writing this paragraph. These were four precious children ages 9,11,12,&13. God had placed them in my womb for ME TO CARE FOR and yet they would be shuffled around from place to place. I led a selfish life and even though in my heart I knew I really loved them, I did not raise them as God had intended. God's perfect plan is for us to give our love and devotion to Him, and then train our children to LOVE THE LORD OUR GOD.

For us to not only say we love the Lord but to live a consistent Christian lifestyle as an example for them. This I would not do until they were teenagers. So they went through many lonely times without their mother. I'M SORRY PATTI, BOBBY, PEGGY AND DEE. As you read this book, I've told you before, but I want to publicly say it again. Thank you for forgiving me. You are such a joy in my life, as well as all my precious grandchildren.

CHAPTER SIX
DIVORCED AND DESPERATE
- FROM STRIP DANCING TO OWNING A STRIP BUSINESS -

We became a FRAGMENTED FAMILY! After the DIVORCE the four children stayed with me for a while. Roy paid child support and the bills were paid for a while. Then he fell off a ladder at work and was temporarily on disability. We were renting a nice three-bedroom home with a fireplace and nice yard in a good neighborhood. My comfortable living with nice material things started to crumble. Roy had been a good provider and husband and I never appreciated what I had. The grass truly looks greener on the other side.

I was soon to find myself back to square one before I met him. Without a good man, I was broke, lonely, and living way below standards I had come to know.

This would become an emotionally hard time for my precious children. They would be split up and bounced back and forth between Roy, my parents, and myself. They would eventually not live with me at all for long periods of time. My good intentions were to quickly round them all up when I got financially stable and we'd be together again. I never set out to give them up, but what happened to us can happen to anybody. Days turned into weeks, then months, until suddenly years had passed and their young years were gone. I loved them so much but my search for the American dream let the devil keep me in a spiritual rut, destroying all of our lives.

I was searching for love in all the wrong places and faces. Everyone pursues happiness only to find that without God to fill that empty void in our life, we're on a dead-end street. With no one to be accountable to, we're just like a rebellious teenager. LIFE REALLY GOT OUT OF CONTROL. Self-pity, blaming everyone for my problems, bitterness, and a hard heart were the elements of my character. They had resided with me since my teen years. Here I was now 31 years old, DIVORCED, mother of four, and I couldn't pay my bills. At first, I hit the bars every night of the week, drinking heavily. I was a bartender and cocktail waitress for awhile, doing anything I could to make money. I was sleeping with more men than I can remember. I hated being lonely with no arms around me. Roy had been affectionate until the end when bitterness and fighting got so bad. I missed that. So often a person doesn't appreciate the good things in life until they're gone. I found out that if there is no love or commitment, those arms around you mean nothing. I was EMPTY! In the beginning, I didn't crave sex - I just wanted arms around me. Later on though, that's what I started looking for and began to realize this too would become an ADDICTION. A spirit of LUST had come over me. I was USING OTHERS AND BEING USED! The devil laughs as we're caught in his terrible web. It's a miracle I didn't get a disease.

During this time, Roy was so kind to give me gas money to go to Tennessee to see my daddy. I hadn't seen him for 15 years. That's how long I carried the hate inside me. I know now only God could have lifted this from me even though I wasn't saved at the time. I took all of my kids, Patti, Bobby, Peggy and Dee with me.

He didn't know he had four grandchildren and of course he had never had seen them. After visiting his tiny run down house, we took a ride to Missouri to see relatives. On the way during our conversation I said, "DADDY I FORGIVE YOU for what you did to me as a little child growing up". He got so furious that I said that that he began to curse and deny it. He even tried to jump out of the car while I was driving. I calmed him down and to this day I know God was in that car giving me the grace not to lose my usually nasty temper and react like I normally would. I wasn't but God helps even unsaved people. If He doesn't, I wouldn't be alive and a Christian today.

It hurt tremendously that he didn't acknowledge his sin. I believe that's how God feels when we won't acknowledge our sin against Him. When I came back to see my dad, that hate was completely gone and all I felt was pity. He was a miserable, lonely, old man with no children, grandchildren, wife or parents in his life. That's all I saw - I WAS FREE! God did for me what I couldn't do for myself. I just didn't recognize it at the time, but the Lord was helping me. THANK YOU LORD! HATE AND BITTERNESS had eaten away at my gut for years. If you're feeling that way toward anyone, LET GO AND LET GOD forgive you! What a relief not to carry that anymore!

Four years later DADDY WOULD DIE. I was a Christian then and attended his funeral in Missouri. I took two of my children with me, Bobby and Peggy and his grandson, Brandon. I was sure glad that God destined that time previously and took the hate from me. I gave a mini sermon sharing my testimony at the funeral. I didn't want to bring up the incest and I couldn't share anything good about daddy, I talked about my HEAVENLY DADDY. My aunt was screaming at the top of her lungs uncontrollably, "HE'S IN HELL, HE'S IN HELL!" She had been to the hospital to witness to him many times, and even talked to him a half hour before he died. The doctor said that after she left he died of a heart attack while in the restroom. In the first chapter of this book I wrote that my first memory of daddy was him messing with me while I was using the restroom. Tears are streaming down my face at this realization. I truly hope daddy asked JESUS into his heart before he died. I WANT TO SEE HIM IN HEAVEN!

I was no better than my daddy as far as sin goes. The same devil that enticed me all through my life is the same devil that destroyed his life. Sin is sin. Everybody hates child molesters and it is a terrible evil but Jesus loves them and died for them as well. He died for the whole world (John 3:16).

I remember that the Holy Spirit was my divine counselor one afternoon after I'd been saved about 6 months. I said Lord, "Why did you allow my daddy to have incest with me, an innocent child?" I heard a small, still voice in my mind remind me that everyone has a free will and that God cannot force his will upon anyone. I began to think about how my free will had hurt so many people. We both let the evil one USE US to bring devastation to not only our lives but also so many others. We did not have THE HOLY SPIRIT to give us the power to overcome.

JESUS died to give us the power and authority over those evil spirits. That's why I'm exposing the devil. When people are aware of this spiritual battle, they'll come to understand why they ACT AND THINK like they do. Then you can know where to turn for help and your life CAN BE CHANGED. When YOU KNOW THE TRUTH about JESUS and the BLOOD THAT HE SHED FOR YOU, YOU CAN BE SET FREE! YOU WILL BE FREE INDEED! The CHOICE is up to us. All we have to do is CHOOSE GOD instead of the devil and then the power of the HOLY SPIRIT comes to enable you to keep that choice with a whole heart commitment. We will have no excuse when we die someday and see JESUS face to face. The one who loves us and died for us is waiting to set us free. WE CAN LIVE VICTORIOUSLY - there's no excuse for sin now. "The DEVIL MADE ME DO IT" won't cut it. Jesus will show us his nail scarred hands and say, "MY BLOOD WAS SHED FOR YOU". No temporary pleasure or sin will be worth losing your soul over. Don't let the devil mess with your time here on earth anymore. Jesus has a great PURPOSE AND PLAN for our lives. Jesus has a BETTER LIFE waiting. All we have to do is CHOOSE JESUS and we CHOOSE LIFE.

During those months of heavy drinking I was really hitting bottom. I'd drink for two days straight without eating and sleeping. GAMBLING on the pool table was always a driving force. I couldn't keep appointments. My life was filled with missed family outings and broken promises to the kids. Time meant nothing to me as days swept by in this alcoholic stupor.

I had been dating a guy who was just like me. One day he called from a government-run alcohol and drug treatment center. He was in detox and said that they also took women there if I wanted to sign myself in. At first I thought, "I'm not an ALCOHOLIC - no way". I felt my real problem was loneliness, divorce, bills, stress, etc. I didn't picture myself as the stereotypical alcoholic lying on the street. I just thought this would all pass once I found my dream life. I didn't stop to think that I already had possessed that but had thrown it away because of the alcohol. That's the insanity, doing the same thing over, but expecting different results. I told him that I didn't need that. After a few days though with more bad experiences, I called the nurse and asked if I could join the program. I stayed 5 days for the program, turning down the additional 14 more days they offered.

They gave me a book with spiritual steps in it. I agreed with step one that my life was unmanageable and that I was powerless over alcohol. I even admitted I was an ALCOHOLIC. I wasn't sure about step two as it involved talking to GOD. I wasn't sure if there was a GOD. So they told me to read the agnostic chapter. The Bible says the devil has blinded our eyes from seeing the truth. I couldn't come to grips with that truth though. When I look back I see that if I had believed that truth that it would have made me accountable for ALL my actions, not just the alcohol. I really wasn't ready for step three which was to make a DECISION to TURN MY LIFE AND MY WILL OVER TO THE CARE OF GOD. I was alright with turning over my alcohol problem but didn't want to turn over my SEX LIFE, GAMBLING, CURSING, PORNOGRAPHY, and every other evil I enjoyed. I would not accept this until a few MORE WASTED YEARS.

Without completing steps 2 & 3, I was right back out there letting the devil USE AND ABUSE ME. My poor children and family continued to suffer. Alcoholism and Drug Addiction has a ripple affect where everyone suffers. Our lives do influence others, either for good or evil.

I don't think even a year went by before I called to go back to the program. I was confused, looking for answers to straighten my life out. I guess I thought they could fix it but I know now they're a channel to point to the existence of a GOD, WHO CAN. I was hurting from past failures in relationships and had no hope for a good future.

I felt worthless, and hated myself and others who'd abused me. I lost my self-respect, and wondered about my identity. I had no goals and felt very lonely. I felt safe locked up there (some people in jail have those same feelings) I felt safe from my own self-destructiveness since I wasn't exposed to it there. I was afraid that when I left that I would start back towards the same lifestyle when I got lonely, stressed or angered. I NEEDED A CHANGE. NO CHANGE WOULD COME THEN. I know why now. I wasn't willing to SURRENDER ALL.

God is looking for people who will make a whole heart dedication to live for Him. Would you want to be married to someone who only said they loved you with their lips and their heart was far from you? Most of us have been in relationships where WE or OUR PARTNER, DID AS WE PLEASED and it didn't work. God is a jealous God (the first COMMANDMENT) and He doesn't want us to put ANYTHING or ANYBODY above Him.

Most of us won't let go of that old garbage. We're afraid that we won't have any fun and life will be boring. WRONG! Once you SURRENDER ALL, you'll wonder why you waited so long and you won't miss any of that GARBAGE OF SIN. I'll tell you later on how all those OLD FEELINGS vanished when I FINALLY SURRENDERED ALL.

I was DIVORCED AND DESPERATE. Desperate is a good word to describe how I felt at that time in my life. Bills piled up and I had moved in with my mom and step-dad. Thank God for those precious Godly loved ones, who showed me God's unconditional love. The kids were split between us, our HOME had been WRECKED. I DESPERATELY needed money to get us our own place where we could all live together again.

I searched the want ads for a job. Since real estate is based on commission, that was not my answer. I needed steady reliable money. With no other training and job skills other than my G.E.D., I was getting DESPERATE. In Illinois, rent and utilities are not cheap. As a single mom, I just didn't see how I was going to survive.

I spotted an ad in the newspaper for an EXOTIC DANCER in a nightclub. I thought I'd go check this out since this was a job I definitely had experience in. I was 31 yrs. old at this time. I was impressed at first with this huge club with its big stage and elaborate curtains. They showed me the dressing rooms upstairs and it all appeared glamorous. When we talked about the pay I readily accepted. Boy, I didn't know what I was getting myself into. Before I left he told me this would be slightly different than the type of dancing I'd done previously. This was FULL STRIP, COMPLETE NUDITY for the last few minutes of my performance. He also told me I'd not only get a nightly rate of pay but would get commission on bottles of grape juice which they called champagne. Now I was used to hustling drinks in my past but this would be more degrading. He showed me the darkened back room where you'd sit with the customers who would spend BIG MONEY on bottles of so called champagne. It was terrible. I hated BEING USED like that. Eventually I learned to play the so-called game by HARDENING MY HEART. I got an attitude that I would take them for every penny they had, and use their entire credit card limit if I could. They didn't care about me and I would look at them the same way. I WOULD SURVIVE and get all the money I could get.

  I hated to go to work every night. I acquired more sugar daddies (prostitution without a pimp) which I met during the day. I was a high price CALL GIRL. Since I wasn't cheap, I had a sense of power over these men. I now started smoking marijuana more than ever. I had fallen off stage once when I was drunk and risked losing my job. So I substituted my main drug of choice, even though I still drank. I drank mixed drinks instead as I rationalized beer and shots were my downfall. I felt I needed something to dull my mind to what I was doing, to desensitize me to my surroundings. I needed that TEMPORARY PEACE to deal with this X-RATED LIFESTYLE.

  The other dancers were fuzz brained as well. This was a job nobody wanted to do clear-headed. Everyone had their own type of drug or alcohol they needed to BE ABLE TO COPE. The MONEY is what draws and keeps us poor women into this deep pit. Some who read this may have no pity for strippers or prostitutes. I do because I was one. You never know what brought them to this situation. I now know that the devil is the influence behind it all. JESUS loves all people who are caught up in any type of sin. When anyone learns the TRUTH, and asks JESUS to forgive them and they turn their back on sin in repentance, they WILL NEVER BE THE SAME. The old X-RATED LIFESTYLE will be forgiven and G-RATED (GODLY) LIFESTYLE can be lived. I'M PROOF!

I remember one Sunday morning mom and my step dad asked me to church. I was living with them at the time and accepted. Probably out of feeling I should since they were giving me a place to live. During worship I started crying so badly I walked out and sat in the car. I just sat there and bawled. I remember thinking I wish I could be like all those GOOD PEOPLE. I reasoned that I couldn't and I needed that BIG MONEY to put my family back together.

I realize now that the devil was lying to me. THE HOLY SPIRIT was calling me and that's why I was crying. As far as wanting to be like all those GOOD PEOPLE, they had been sinners at one time, too, before God changed them. Yes, they may not have been at the depths of sin as I had but sin is sin with God. They were only GOOD now because they had taken on the righteousness of God through the BLOOD OF JESUS. I know now that not all people who sit in the church are saved. There are many who have some type of sin in their life that God is dealing with them about. Some church members and even those in ministry are not living a consistent holy G-RATED (GODLY) LIFESTYLE. Years later I would BACKSLIDE and experience that terrible spiritual battle for my soul. I now have compassion for others stuck in that spiritual rut.

I continued to dance in the nightclub for quite awhile. It sickened me though and it really brought my self-esteem to an all-time low so I eventually quit. About a week later that club was busted. Wow, I could have been there and went to jail.

I now had a steady boyfriend who was about 10 years younger than me. One of his friends was about to get married and asked me if I'd dance at his BACHELOR PARTY. He said that he would pay me $150.00 for a half hour. That was real good money 20 years ago and nothing to sneeze at now. I said OK but my boyfriend would be my bodyguard and there'd be no touching. So off we went that night with my big boom box, elaborate costumes and props. I made lots of tips along with that

150.00. I gave my boyfriend a small portion and I kept the rest. I was excited. To me this was great, a dream job. I got to do what I loved to do - DANCE. Best of all there was no grubby paws touching me. I viewed this as entertainment now and felt self-worth.

That evening was a huge TURNING POINT in my life. This destructive choice would set me on a course of not only EVIL but a SUCCESSFUL X-RATED LIFESTYLE. I always had a mind for business that developed through my short real estate career. I had been good at school and would soon put that knowledge to WORK FOR THE DEVIL. God gives us talents and abilities that He desires for us to use to further His Kingdom. Unfortunately, many of us use these to further the devil's work. I would BE USED AND USE OTHERS to an even greater extent.

After that evening the devil inspired me to get business cards and start an actual business doing this. It was very profitable and I soon discovered that it was viewed as good entertainment in the world's eyes.

I called my business, "KANDI ROSE PRODUCTIONS". I felt I was actually producing good clean fun. I guess I thought it was clean because there was no touching and prostitution involved. How ridiculous! I was "DANCING FOR THE DEVIL". Soon, women were asking for male strippers for their bachelorette and birthday parties. So I advertised and held auditions for male strippers. When I went out to regular public nightclubs for a social night out, I'd scout for men and women I COULD USE. See, now not only was the devil USING ME, but I WAS FINDING OTHERS TO BE USED. Face it, you're either going to BE USED as an evil influence or Godly influence in this world. PRAISE GOD, I'M BEING USED BY GOD NOW. The devil won't BE USING ME ANY MORE!

I used to think this was so glamorous and exciting. I was not only looked up to as a celebrity, and entertainer, but now as a talent scout. In a short time I had 26 people working for me. It snowballed from just male and female private strip shows into a Theatrical Booking Agency, where we performed in public nightclubs. I choreographed 2-hour nightclub shows that consisted of all types of entertainment. I had magicians, break dancers, hypnotists, and of course scantily clad dancers, performing skit scenes. I had two men who could dance on roller skates. So I had one dress as a clown and named him ROSE-O (after me) to dance on those skates during intermission. I also did an act as a vampire coming out of a coffin. For the grand finale I did a swan-dive into two of my male dancers arms from a high point off stage. It's hard to believe that I really did those things. I'm SO CHANGED NOW!

    I advertised this business to the hilt. I put ads in the newspapers, yellow pages, magazines, on radio stations, and even a Billboard across the street from a Drive-In Movie. I had a commercial on Cable TV. The commercial had a limo portraying me and my dancers getting out of it, in front of a nightclub. We were all dressed in tuxedos and formal wear. Then it showed the dancers and me in costume, individually dancing. The television station came and televised this on location. This commercial was aired about 40 times a day. It appeared on MTV (music video station), Nashville Network, ESPN (sports network), news networks and several other stations. I also danced on the Lake County Fairgrounds Stage and had a promotional table set up to advertise my business. I joined the Round Lake Chamber of Commerce. I had a promo table set up at The Business and Home Expo.

    I was MS. AUTOFEST at the Arlington Park Race Track for their huge Car Show. About 40,000 people came. I was dressed in a long black evening gown with a white satin banner that read, "MS. AUTOFEST." I awarded about 200 trophies out to the winners of the car show. I had a male and female dancer by my side along with my manager, Katy. I had professional pictures of each of us and we autographed them at my promo table. I was also Lake County's MOST Prominent SHOWGIRL at the Lake County Auto Show. This was held at the Lake County Fairgrounds. I walked around in a bikini, with a parasol, having my picture taken by numerous antique and muscle cars. I awarded trophies and signed autographs. Another similar situation was the

McHenry Boat and Auto Show where there were trophies, autographs, and pictures taken again.

A well known worldwide charitable organization that holds picnics and auctions every year for a fundraiser used me as an item to bid on. I stood in front of the auctioneer in formal wear while he held bids for one of my performances. The wives of a rescue squad bid 150.00 for me to do a full strip for their husbands during the day at the rescue station.   When my boyfriend and I broke up, my best friend, Katy, became my manager and bodyguard. She'd stand with me by the door or near me with her one hand inside her coat. They would ask if she had a gun and she'd just smile. She told me after I got saved that she prayed lots of times when we were in some very evil situations. I know now GOD DID HAVE ANGELS GUARDING US. Katy always acted tough and I credited our safety to my attitude of being in control and setting the crowd straight beforehand. THANK YOU LORD! I tell you the devil can give you boldness to do or go into some very dangerous situations. As a Christian we need to let God use us to do or go wherever there are lost sheep to rescue.

On three different occasions we volunteered to work fundraisers for our local town Chamber of Commerce's. These were golf fundraisers. We hopped on the booze golf cart, dressed in my bikini and parasol. Katy drove and I would stand when I could and dance. Once she drove under a tree and a branch that almost got me. I enjoyed fundraisers. I felt I was doing a good deed and was also getting advertisement as well.

During the Christmas season, Katy and I went to the North Chicago VA Hospital. I dressed in costume and danced up and down the hallways popping into rooms, handing out candy. On one occasion one of my male dancers put on a sequined costume and danced on roller skates in and out and around the seniors who were sitting at tables. I also danced in a white beaded costume.

I'll never forget what my born again friend, Lily, said to me as I bragged about this event. She said, "that was great that you wanted to make them smile and be happy but God wants you to give them something that will last forever – JESUS!" I now know what she meant! Ever since I got saved, I no longer promote self, I PROMOTE JESUS!

Yes, I was having fun doing all this. Katy and I would cut up and joke, all the while counting the money. I loved to dance and was respected and recognized in the upper class business world. Even wives and girlfriends were hiring my dancers and me. I even danced in the basement of one of the local town police stations. I was hired by one of the police officers for another officer's party. The wife of a wealthy funeral home owner had me come to their house for her husband's birthday party. I dressed as a vampire and came out of one of their coffins. There were so many unusual places and people that used my services; this is only to name a few.

Sin is pleasurable for a season. That means it's fun for just a short time. Afterward, however, there's an empty feeling. I wasn't feeling guilt or shame at this time – I was proud of who I was – but I had NO PEACE, NO CONTENTMENT, AND NO SERENITY! SOMETHING WAS MISSING! I thought it was because I didn't have a steady guy or my children with me. Now I know what was missing: THE TRUE LOVE OF MY LIFE - JESUS!

I remember a few times that a particular thought would cross my mind. The thought was, "What if I do become Lake County's richest woman (because I was headed that way) and still die and GO TO HELL?" I didn't know it then there's a verse in the Bible that talks about that that (Matthew 16:26). I hadn't ever read that scripture so I know God was talking to me.

After the glamour of the day would fade, I'd lay on my bed just restless. I COULDN'T SLEEP. I'd smoke pot to try and relieve stress. I'd light up almost every hour from the time I woke up until I went to bed. I didn't want my buzz to fade a bit. I had become addicted to pot instead of alcohol because I couldn't run my business drunk all the time.

Late hours were spent under the influence of pot which I thought was the reason for my awesome creativity in advertising techniques. Satan gives creative abilities that are very successful.

Just look at Hollywood producing such evil content through movies, music and magazines. There is an abundance of SEX, VIOLENCE AND LANGUAGE that sickens both GOD and ME. R-RATED AND X-RATED productions are made that LEAD US INTO TEMPTATION. BEWARE of what you SEE, HEAR, OR READ. Guard your soul. God gives us the ability to choose. CHOOSE FREEDOM THROUGH CHRIST, not slavery to LUST AND PORNOGRAPHY as I once did.

I now CHOOSE to be under the inspiration of THE HOLY SPIRIT to be creative for The LORD. That's why I'm writing this book. That's why I also evangelize using illustrated sermons through characters such as: LIL' BO PEEP, BRIDE OF CHRIST, THE GOOD NEWS ANGEL, and now, SHEPHERD'S ROSE. God is a creator and we are made in His image. He's given creative ability to be used by Him or the devil. IT'S OUR CHOICE. I CHOOSE THE LORD - HOW ABOUT YOU?

I'd be up all hours of the night. My mind would not shut down and let my body sleep. Smoking pot usually relaxed me but I found that there was no REST FOR THE WICKED. I felt such emptiness. I found myself picking up a Bible that mom had given me. I began to read bits and pieces of the book of PSALMS. This whole book was foreign to me but after reading a little, my mind would be at peace and I'd be able to sleep. I knew there was something different about that book.

I was unaware that God was drawing me towards knowing him. He knew I WAS LOST and had compassion on me. He had created me when I was in my mother's womb (Psalm 139). He had been there all through those years of pain and hurt. Nevertheless, He saw me as valuable, precious, and special in His eyes. I was one of the millions upon millions HE DIED FOR.
I WAS ABOUT TO BE FOUND!!!!!!!

CHAPTER SEVEN
THE CHOICE THAT AFFECTED MY DESTINY
- VICTORY OVER EVIL! -

Is there an INVISIBLE, UNSEEN, and SPIRITUAL REALM that influences our CHOICES? Are there DEMONS and a DEVIL? Is there a GOD, JESUS, HOLY SPIRIT, and ANGELS? Do OUR CHOICES have CONSEQUENCES determine OUR DESTINY? Is there a SPIRITUAL BATTLE of GOOD and EVIL influencing OUR CHOICES that will ultimately lead to OUR DESTINY?

Well I'm convinced that all of these exist. As you read this chapter, I believe you will too. Review your own past choices and ponder certain occasions that you thought were just lucky, unlucky, or just coincidence. I do believe there was an EVIL INFLUENCE that played havoc with my life. I also believe there is a GOD who INTERVENED on my behalf many times through this SPIRITUAL REALM. While writing this book, I'm overwhelmed at GOD'S LOVE and MERCY.

My mom, step dad, children, friends and others can definitely attest to this SPIRITUAL MIRACLE. I say MIRACLE because when you've tried to CHANGE YOURSELF as many times as I did in years past, you know that you know, it's SUPERNATURAL. The MULTIPLE ADDICTIONS, the HARD HEART, the BITTER ATTITUDE, none of them CHANGED through my OWN WILL POWER.

Certain addictions, habits and attitudes I would abstain from. Sometimes I would be clean from them for days, weeks and even months but then return to them - usually to a worse condition than before. This book is being PUBLISHED in 2005 and I now have 16 years abstinence from ALL ADDICTIONS and now have a soft loving heart with a definite attitude adjustment. Not bragging on my self because SELF didn't CHANGE SELF. *GOD DID IT!!!!!!*

A SPIRITUAL BATTLE for my soul was about to be won in the HEAVENLIES. About a week before being saved, my mom had a horrendous nightmare. She said she couldn't tell if it was a dream or a vision because it was so real to her. Mom, my step-dad, Lily and countless other Christians from various churches were bombarding heaven on my behalf. It's called intercessory prayer, or standing in the gap for someone. This one particular evening mom said she had this vision/dream of me being put naked in a large wicker basket with two beings trying to cram the lid down on my head She also had a perverted vision of me which sickened her with disgust.

Now my mom's ministry is intercessory prayer. Even though she has suffered so much physically in her body all her life with different ailments, she has had such compassion for lost and hurting people. She has unconditional love for all people, including me, and is not critical or judgmental. She realizes she was a sinner and needed JESUS just as much as I did. This woman of God has been in tremendous pain herself from osteo and rheumatoid arthritis plus other afflictions. Through it all, she has always kept the joy of the Lord and looked beyond herself to pray for hundreds of people. PRAYER WORKS and is a MIGHTY MINISTRY in SPIRITUAL BATTLE.

My mom said that for the first time in her life she felt totally appalled and disgusted with my X-RATED LIFESTYLE and me. So much so, she angrily got up and turned my picture around that hung in the dining room. Up to this point, mom had never given up praying for me, although with the natural eye it looked like the devil had me. I'm sure the devil had put it in her thoughts many times that I would never change. Everyone needs to remember to KEEP PRAYING FOR YOUR LOVED ONES. When it's the darkest, THE LIGHT IS COMING! God loves doing the impossible, so that only He can get the credit or GLORY for the MIRACLE.

I certainly was at the most evil condition of my life. I was OUT OF CONTROL, although I didn't think so. I thought I was doing real well and I loved what I was doing. I proclaimed that no one, not even a man could get me to quit what I was doing. That's how much I enjoyed this business. I was determined to be independent, to be the richest woman I could be, and to give my children everything they could want in life.

As soon as mom turned my picture around with such disgust, THE HOLY SPIRIT spoke to her. She recognized the devil's strategy. He was trying to get her to quit praying for me. She got so mad at the devil that she started intense spiritual warfare for me. She rebuked and cast the devil out of my life, pleading the BLOOD OF JESUS over me. She said, "IN THE NAME OF JESUS CHRIST I bind you and command you to loose her and all those evil spirits have to leave NOW, IN JESUS NAME!"

Well, I tell you, PRAYER WORKS. My deliverance was set in motion through this SPIRITUAL BATTLE. THE HOLY SPIRIT and the ANGELS were dispatched on my behalf and about a week later I WAS DELIVERED FROM THOSE EVIL SPIRITS, SAVED AND SET FREE. A series of events was taking place to orchestrate my deliverance and salvation. NOTHING IS COINCIDENCE!

A short time prior to this taking place, two ministers, brother Paul and brother Wayne from Lily's church, felt compelled to go to my business office parking lot to pray for my salvation.

They were confident God would save me but they had no idea I was soon to become a member of their tiny church, not my mom's. They would also become two of the greatest male mentors in my life. Their ministries would impact my life to help me walk the walk for a G-RATED (GODLY) LIFESTYLE.

People came up to me later from various churches that didn't know my family or me and said that they had prayed for me. They had stretched their hands out to my huge Billboard and asked God to close that business and save the people. WOW!

Lil and I knew each other from bowling and never really hung out with each other. Even though at the time we were not real close friends, God began to give her such a compassion for my soul. Mom and her had become good friends as they had the same heavenly Father. She continued to stop by the bowling alley and witness to me. She was very UNLIKE me. She was not a drinker or wild person. She was a quiet housewife who'd been married as a teen to the same man all her life. Yet she didn't judge me. God gave her compassion for me as a lost sheep that needed THE GOOD SHEPHERD. She did what Christians are supposed to do, PRAY AND WITNESS.

Lil had asked me a couple of times to come to her church but I always said, MAYBE, ONE OF THESE DAYS. Then suddenly I found myself saying YES on a Monday night, March 4, 1984.

The funny thing was that on that very night I was booked to do a fundraiser. A Lake County Judge that was up for re-election was having a dinner and candlelight bowl at a popular bowling alley. I had donated one of my performances in the form of a coupon as one of the prizes for the bowling winners. Then after the dinner during their cocktail hour I brought a male and female dancer with me to perform a skit scene (not a strip but in scanty costumes). I had just started to date a recovering alcoholic who I really liked and he was my date that night.

I forgot that I had this booking when I agreed to go to church (GOD KNEW THOUGH). After the show was over, I looked at my watch and thought I was a half hour late and almost didn't go. If I'd known I was that late I wouldn't have even gone. That old saying, BETTER LATE THAN NEVER really applied to me then.   I told my date we were going to church and since I drove, he had no way of not going. It's funny now to think about what an unusual date this would be for him: we started the evening X-RATED and would finish it G-RATED. I doubt if anyone has had this type of dating experience.

As I was driving there these thoughts were going on in my mind. WHY ARE YOU GOING TO CHURCH? YOU JUST CAME FROM DOING A SHOW!! LOOK AT WHO YOU ARE? A STRIPPER AND OWNER OF A STRIP BUSINESS!! THIS IS CRAZY!! Well I know now that our choices are INFLUENCED by EVIL SPIRITS to keep us from OUR PURPOSE AND DESTINY.

Lil said they'd been having a REVIVAL, and a former gang member and drug addict from Chicago was preaching, so it sparked my interest. When we walked in, brother John was preaching up a storm. My date and I slipped into the back pew. I felt real weird. I had a long fur coat over a slinky purple satin jumpsuit, silver high heels, big floppy velvet hat and purple satin choker on my neck. I left my coat on though, I definitely was not dressed like these church folks were. Matter of fact I must have been standing out like a sore thumb. Although I noticed only smiling faces. We had just smoked some marijuana on the way there and still had some left in my purse.

The evangelist, brother John, was a very loud and excited preacher. He was so passionate for Christ. I remember thinking about what a CHANGE GOD HAD MADE IN THIS MAN. I also saw a true joy and enthusiasm he had for lost souls. True joy was something I didn't have. Yes, my business and dancing was a so-called joy but this was different. I saw him cry and plead for people to be saved.

Since we were an hour late we missed a lot of the message. Nevertheless, THE HOLY SPIRIT starting talking to me immediately. He was URGING me to SURRENDER my life over to Jesus. Brother John came back to our pew and said, GOD HAS A MIRACLE FOR YOU. There were other words God said to me through him, but this is the phrase I remember. I didn't get saved that night because I QUICKLY EXITED the church. I was very uncomfortable and uneasy. Who do you think was making me feel that way? I know now. Once we got in the car, something strange happened. I found myself scanning the radio for a preaching station. I had NEVER, NEVER done anything like that before. I always had my radio tuned to the latest top hits as loud as I could crank it and kind of dancing in my seat as I drove. This was a real switch.

As we lit up a joint of pot we discussed if there was a possibility that God existed. I realize now that THE LORD was revealing himself to me and I was beginning to awake spiritually. The Bible says that we can't come to Him unless THE HOLY SPIRIT draws us. This was the first of A SERIES OF EVENTS that started happening prior to my salvation. The next event that would happen would become the best night of my life. IT WAS *THE CHOICE THAT AFFECTED MY DESTINY!!*

The revival had been on a Monday evening. Tuesday they had revival again but I didn't go. After their service that evening, Lil, some church folks, the Pastor and evangelist John, went to a nearby restaurant. I had recently moved my office to Katy and Will's basement. That evening I received a devastating phone call that was more than I could bear. I thought that two of my children were going to be put into a foster home. I could handle almost anything in life but this was my rock bottom. I was hysterical and needed PEACE of mind to deal with this - *HERE'S GOD'S PERFECT TIMING!*

Immediately after that alarming phone call, the phone rang again. It was Lily calling from the restaurant to see if I wanted to join them. I was crying and said no thanks. Lil told me later that she didn't really want to call me (she's so shy) but felt THE HOLY SPIRIT strongly urge her to get up and call. This was strange indeed since we never really socialized together except for bowling. For her to call for anything, much less to call this time of night was very odd.

After I hung up the phone a SPIRITUAL BATTLE took place for my heart, mind and soul, right there in my office. I was so distraught. My heart was so hard that not much could bother me. When it came to my kids, God knew this was an area that was dear to me. Even though from all appearances it looked like I didn't care because of my lifestyle. God knew my motivation was to make money so my kids and I could get back together. Sin was KEEPING ME LONGER THAN I WANTED TO STAY. It will keep you longer than you expect as time slips away, day after day, week after week, year after year. Soon sin has actually kept us with BROKEN DREAMS and BROKEN PROMISES to everyone involved.

Remember the cartoon years back that showed an ANGEL on one shoulder, telling the cartoon character to do good? Then on the other shoulder a pitchfork guy telling him to do bad? Well that's the best way I can describe this INVISIBLE BATTLE for my mind, heart, and soul. THE HOLY SPIRIT was telling me to give me life to Jesus so that I could finally know true peace and forgiveness. The EVIL SPIRITS were telling me to not be foolish and throw away my business and my chance to be rich. Besides, I LOVED TO DANCE.

It was a hard DECISION as I really enjoyed my new found career. People were admiring and respecting me like a Hollywood entertainer. Everywhere I went people were recognizing me from the COMMERCIALS and PERSONAL APPEARANCES. Still, there was an emptiness and a void in my life. I thought it was because I hadn't met my dream man or hadn't gotten my kids back yet. I had forgotten that I had both of those things at one time and I still wasn't satisfied then. You have to see that people, places and things can't give you TRUE SERENITY. We were made to have an INTIMATE RELATIONSHIP with God through His Son, JESUS CHRIST. Many people say that they have peace, but if there is unrepented sin in their lives, the devil is just deceiving them. GOD IS HOLY and we must live a G-RATED (GODLY) LIFESTYLE, in order to be INTIMATE with Him. Since we were born with a sinful nature, God sent His son, JESUS, to die for us so we could have the POWER to BE ABLE TO SAY NO to sin. It's His BLOOD shed on Calvary's Cross that makes us Holy. It's our CHOICE to accept the Good News and be willing to TURN FROM OUR OLD LIFESTYLE no matter what.

While I was in this SPIRITUAL BATTLE that was calling for a DECISION, I called my mom. My oldest daughter, Patti, answered and was about 16 at the time. She was living with my mom and step dad. I started telling her what had just transpired. I was using her as a sounding board while I told her about the CROSSROADS I had reached. It was a CROSSROADS that needed a DECISION. I was crying. I needed PEACE desperately. I felt I was losing my mind.

I didn't know what the word repentance meant then but THE HOLY SPIRIT was telling me. He said I'd have to let go of my X-RATED LIFESTYLE. I had tried many times to CHANGE MYSELF and couldn't. At this point GOD was putting that faith in me to believe it WAS POSSIBLE THIS TIME. He was telling me to SURRENDER EVERYTHING. He told me to not worry how it would happen but to have childlike faith to TRUST HIM. Repent means TURN AWAY FROM, go in the other direction, and make a U-TURN. That's what so AMAZING about being SAVED - WE DON'T DO IT!! *IT'S A MIRACLE FROM GOD!*

All we have to do is make a SINCERE, WHOLE HEART COMMITMENT (really mean it) and LET HIM BE IN CONTROL OF OUR LIFE. We aren't just to TALK IT but to WALK IT.

After a few minutes of mulling THIS HARD DECISION over with my daughter, I asked her to put mom on the phone. I was crying so hard and said mom, I WANT TO GIVE MY LIFE TO JESUS!! She started crying with tears of joy as you can imagine and said that she would lead me in a prayer to confess my sins and I WOULD BE SAVED (Romans 10:9-10). I don't remember the exact words but GOD HEARD and He knew that I REALLY MEANT IT.

This is the BIGGEST MIRACLE OF ALL, one that can't be seen with the natural, physical eye. THE HOLY SPIRIT actually comes into your body. We become the temple for GOD to live in and work through. It's God who gives us the POWER AND ABILITY to LIVE a G-RATED LIFE because we now are His redeemed child (John 1:12).

WOW! When that prayer ended a PEACE came over me like I've never known before. I've got tears in my eyes as I recall that night. I KNEW THAT I NOW BELONGED TO GOD. He was MY HEAVENLY DADDY and everything was going to be alright. Childlike faith was there. Just as a little child doesn't worry about tomorrow or the future, I didn't either.

After we prayed, I said, "Mom, could you call Lil at the restaurant and see if they'd open the church doors, so I can go in and pray?" She said that she'd call me right back. GUESS WHAT? They were still there and said they'd meet me at the church. I asked mom if she'd go. She was crying with joy as she agreed. I headed out to pick her up since she didn't drive.

Well I was so excited, full of anticipation. You'd thought I'd won a million dollars. Better yet, I had just met THE LOVE

OF MY LIFE, JESUS. I searched my closet for something decent to put on. Everything I owned was sexy, tight and revealing. I found a low cut dress and safety pinned the neck. For once in my life, I wanted to be modest and NOT EXPOSE MYSELF. That was a MIRACLE right there, if you'd known me before (and I'm modest to this day). My eyes truly were opened. I started to recognize good and evil and no longer wanted evil in my life. Just prior to all this happening I had been smoking pot. MY MIND WAS CLEAR now and I DIDN'T EVEN WANT to smoke anymore. I usually lit up every 45 minutes or hour, non-stop throughout the day.

When I got in the car to go get mom, I started to light a cigarette. Now I smoked two packs of cigarettes a day for 24 years, a chain smoker. Here's another SPIRITUAL BATTLE. The voice of THE LORD said, "Come all the Way." Needless to say I was getting another message of why not to do it. Well I obeyed GOD'S VOICE and rolled down the window and threw them out. Lighter included since I wouldn't be smoking pot or cigarettes. I haven't smoked for the last 20 years. MORE FREEDOM!!

I want you to know that I had such an excitement stirring within me that when I got to mom's we were both laughing and crying at the same time. Finally had tears of JOY!! It was probably around 11 pm when we got to the church and somewhere around midnight before we left. When we entered that church I literally ran to the altar and fell down crying. I was so aware of HIS HOLY PRESENCE. I held my hands to the neck of that dress to make sure I wasn't exposed. For the first time in my life I truly felt shame and guilt for the life I had led. I used to be so brazen and hard hearted but now in HIS HOLY PRESENCE I saw myself for who I really was. I told God how truly sorry I was and confessed all my sins. I cried and cried at the realization that I had wasted the life He had given me. Then PEACE came over me as he spoke to my heart and mind. I knew in my spirit that He loved me and I was totally forgiven. I experienced at that moment as I still do today, the fullness of JOY IN HIS PRESENCE that the Bible talks about. There is LOVE,

FORGIVENESS AND POWER when you learn to trust Him. I am still amazed today at His Great Love and Mercy for us, HIS SHEEP. He truly is A GOOD SHEPHERD who SEEKS OUT THE LOST ones. I'm glad He found me. I'm glad I didn't refuse WHEN HE CALLED ME.

When I got up from that altar the old KANDI ROSE was gone. The old life was put to death and I was risen with Christ to a NEW LIFE. The X-RATED LIFESTYLE was buried and the G-RATED LIFESTYLE was resurrected. I not only found PEACE, but I found a personal relationship with a RISEN SAVIOR, JESUS CHRIST. He is my closest intimate companion, who has always been there for me. I never realized all those years that He had already destined me to become like Him. I know now what the Bible verse, *"cast all your care upon me"* means. When I got up from that altar, I didn't have a worry or care, I gave it all to the LORD JESUS. What a feeling! It's hard to describe it, but to those who have also met JESUS, you understand. I felt no shame or guilt, he'd forgiven me! I felt very LOVED and SPECIAL to think that He would reveal Himself to me, a STRIPPER, PROSTITUE AND ADDICT. After I read the Bible, I understand that people just like me are who he died for – SINNERS. Sin of any kind, no matter how big or little it may appear, cannot enter into HEAVEN because GOD IS A HOLY GOD. We all need forgiveness and that's what the CROSS and HIS SHED BLOOD are all about. I WAS LOST but NOW I AM FOUND!

The next day I was on the phone calling downtown Chicago telling them I was saved and to take my huge Billboard down. I remember the day it was put up. Katy and I sat in front of it amazed and excited, knowing this would make us rich. Now, it disgusted me and being rich was unimportant compared to this new life I now had with JESUS. My whole mindset about my business completely turned around. I saw it as evil now and wanted no part of it. I called all of my advertisers, employees, nightclubs etc. and dissolved that business, as I proudly proclaimed to them, I'M SAVED NOW. I was so happy and carefree, even knowing there'd be no more riches and that I was now unemployed. That was all alright because I knew I was in good hands. GOD WAS IN CONTROL, NOT ME, ANYMORE.

I didn't crave any of those addictions anymore either. I only craved HIS PRESENCE, HIS WORD, CHURCH, OTHER CHRISTIANS, PRAYING AND WITNESSING. IT WAS AWESOME!! GOD'S Spirit in me MADE THE DIFFERENCE. HE brought about THE CHANGE. I only had to be willing.

Very shortly after, I moved in with mom and papa (my step dad). They were my greatest examples and mentors along with Lil. The next evening was a Wednesday and I went back to church with Lil instead of my folks. I felt that her church was where I should be since I had that wonderful meeting with Jesus at that altar. There's no place more special to you than the place that you get saved. It was as though I gave marriage vows to Jesus to LOVE, HONOR AND OBEY HIM. The Bible says that we become one with Christ.

In that little church there were so many loving people who accepted me and made me feel like one of their family. They didn't care about what kind of woman I had been. They were excited to see what a miracle God had done in me.

About a week later, Lil and I were cleaning the church, even the toilets. Here I was, the so called "star of Lake County", cleaning toilets! I was thrilled to do something for the Lord.

This church was different than moms. They didn't believe in wearing pants, shorts, makeup and jewelry - so I didn't. I wanted to please God so much it didn't matter. I now know that God is looking at our heart, actions, and attitudes. It's still pleasing to God to dress modestly though, and Christians should never wear anything that would be an obvious temptation to someone else. It was good for me to have strong restrictions after coming out of such a wild and crazy life.

I was now broke, had no business, and no job. It was good because I got to experience GOD AS MY PROVIDER. Nothing is coincidence or luck. God uses people to meet our needs and makes opportunities arise for employment. My first job was as a nanny, watching 3 children. What a switch huh? I made in a week what I used to make in a half hour. I was so contented though. Money was no longer an issue or priority .About six months later, I got asked to manage the world's largest Salvation Army Thrift Store.

By the way, I didn't have to put the kids in a foster home. God worked that out right away. I didn't go back on my vow to God though, like I used to. Lots of times we say, "God if you'll do this or that, then I'll live for you", but so often we don't fulfill our promises. I knew by the circumstances surrounding my conversion that there was definitely a God caring for me and that I needed to keep my vows to Him. HE IS REAL – He is A SPIRIT. Even though I can't see Him, He's there and has been all my life. He's the one that made good things happen in my life. I call it a "God hook-up". The bad events are a "devil hook-up."

It's important to stay in GOD'S Word, to pray, to be faithful to church, and to share your testimony with those around you. There is a SPIRITUAL BATTLE that takes place everyday of our lives. Everyday we must CHOOSE if we are going to do HIS WILL or ours.

One of the last ADDICTIONS in my life to go was LUST. About 2 weeks after I was saved, I heard a sermon about SAMSON and DELILAH (Judges 16). I had surrendered all my other addictions and sin except FORNICATION (sex outside of marriage). When I heard this sermon, I knew God was talking to me. Here I was at another CROSSROADS. I knew God had given me SUPERNATURAL POWER just as he had Samson. I had personally experienced this for myself, not just from hearing or reading about someone else's life. I knew I didn't produce this kind of power on my own.

The evil one was telling me, God doesn't want you to be alone and lonely. Besides, it's only ONE man, you're not sleeping with anyone else. What a liar he is, to get us to COMPROMISE and lose our intimate relationship with the one who loves us and gave His life for us. This was another SPIRITUAL BATTLE that the Good Shepherd's voice was telling me to surrender ALL THE WAY.

I remember saying, God – don't take away SEX!! I gave you my business, pot, alcohol, pornography, gambling, cursing, even cigarettes but please NOT SEX. I was crying when I left church but had not surrendered during the altar call or the prayer time.

I visited with the evangelist, brother John, the next day. I was very distraught and through tears told him the situation and how I had surrendered all to Jesus except this. I tried rationalizing and minimizing. He said with such compassion after he heard me out, "I'll pray for you to marry a Christian husband." I was so let down. I didn't want to hear that, I wanted to hear how it was good that all the other old garbage was gone and that this would be OK. The Bible clearly states ***"NO FORNICATORS shall inherit the kingdom of God"*** (Galatians 5:19).

I tell you I was totally upset. I felt like going out to commit suicide. That was certainly not God's voice INFLUENCING then. I was crying real hard as I struggled spiritually with the realization that God wanted ABSTINENCE. I DIDN'T WANT TO GIVE IT UP, simple as that, I WASN'T WILLING.

I went home and told my mom. We cried together and God gave her the right words to speak to me. She couldn't lie and tell me what I wanted to hear. The Truth is what SETS US FREE. That truth is in God's Word, THE BIBLE.

I knew I didn't want my old life back. I loved this new relationship with THE LOVE OF MY LIFE, JESUS. I also didn't want those other addictions to come back on me. I didn't want to lose the power I was experiencing and knew I would, just like Samson, if I continued to sleep with this man. Was SEX WORTH LOSING my pure relationship with JESUS? Was it worth LOSING MY PEACE, and JOY and missing HEAVEN? NO!! After all, look what JESUS GAVE UP TO HAVE US, HIS VERY LIFE. He surrendered ALL, COULDN'T I??

Yes, I could. YES I DID! I made another CHOICE that affected my DESTINY. I called my boyfriend and told him. He said that my decision was alright with him and that we could continue to date. I was thrilled. So we went to a bowling ally and shot pool – but not for MONEY!

He talked me into going to a motel room just to watch TV and have a private place to be together. I said OK. Dumb, dumb, dumb. THE HOLY SPIRIT was living in me and was speaking loud and clear when I walked in. It didn't take long and I was bawling. This was a switch for me because I never had a conscience or thought I was doing wrong about anything pertaining to any type of sexual activity. I totally sensed MY HEAVENLY FATHER'S PRESENCE in that room. Not judging, but with loving eyes feeling sorrow for his little girl. The best example I can give to describe that feeling is like this: if you had the most wonderful loving spouse in the world and they were there watching as you were about to be disloyal. Or if your loving parent or grandparent, someone you respected was about to see you engage in sex, right in front of them. This of course even went beyond that. This was THE HOLY ONE, THE ALMIGHTY GOD, who LOVES US and created us for His pleasure. He was right there, as He always was, during all those other times of sexual impurity during my life as well. I just didn't have His Holy Spirit inside me to recognize His existence, prior to this.

I felt so ASHAMED, and ran out of there, glad I hadn't done anything. When I got in the car and sped out of there, it hit me. GOD HELPED ME WIN THAT SPIRITUAL BATTLE. LUST had been defeated by His power, not mine. I started crying again but not from sadness but JOY as I realized what had just happened. VICTORY! I felt so clean and so pure. I realize now I was spiritually a virgin. God had forgiven all my sins, including all the sexual ones as well. AWESOME! I am still moved as I remember what a loving, forgiving, and merciful God He is. You can't tell me that EVIL SPIRITS aren't at work trying to INFLUENCE our CHOICES. Or that THE HOLY SPIRIT isn't trying to lead us to JESUS.

What a MIRACLE that I stayed abstinent for years. Finally I had true self-worth and self-esteem. It doesn't come from a career, material things, or even human relationships. It comes from knowing everything is pure before a holy God. When there's no intentional sin in your life, there's no shame or reluctance to be in His presence. You rest in the fact that you're forgiven, loved and honoring Him. Pleasing God is all I want to do. You can't please people all the time but what's important is pleasing Him.

One example of a true Christian lifestyle is how GOD'S plan for marriage was intended. If you're married to a good and loving spouse, you wouldn't want to do anything bad to destroy that relationship. Sin separates us from a HOLY GOD. It puts up a wall between us, so that we can't have a pure relationship just like addiction puts up a wall in human relationships. In a similar way, we can't straddle the fence and live any way we want. Keeping any type of INTENTIONAL sin no matter how big or small ruins our pure relationship with a HOLY GOD.

My life was definitely X-RATED with lots of EXTREME SIN CONTENT. Even when you think your life is only R-RATED or PG-RATED, SIN IS STILL SIN. No sin will enter Heaven unless we ask God's forgiveness and REPENT.

When we do let our LIFESTYLE be changed by GOD, you'll have greater PEACE and SERENITY than can ever be found in any of the OLD GARBAGE you used to try. It feels great to be forgiven and have a NEW LIFE. No, we don't become perfect, but true Christians don't keep INTENTIONALLY SINNING. When we mess up, we ask GOD'S forgiveness as quickly as possible and He will forgive us (I JOHN 1:9). Don't continually sin on purpose. Repent means to turn away from, to no longer be involved in it in any way.

If YOU would like a LIFESTYLE CHANGE right now, say this PRAYER OUT LOUD AS YOU READ IT:

LORD JESUS CHRIST, I believe that you died on the CROSS for ME. You shed your BLOOD so that I could be forgiven and become YOUR CHILD. I ask THE HOLY SPIRIT to come and live inside of ME. I now CHOOSE to live for you with MY WHOLE HEART. I accept YOUR LOVE, POWER AND FORGIVENESS. I FORGIVE MYSELF and those who have hurt me as well. On the CROSS you defeated

the devil and I CAN HAVE VICTORY IN MY LIFE. I LOVE YOU JESUS!!!!!!!

AMEN!

If you said that prayer and really meant it, you are His Child, you are BORN AGAIN (Romans 10: 9,10). Call someone right now and tell them what has just happened in your life. Find a church that teaches the whole Bible, read your Bible, pray, and start getting to know your new best friend. You are now a brand new person!! (II Cor. 5:17)

Please write me and let me know, too. In a future book I intend to share testimonies of all the LIFESTYLE CHANGES that come about as a result of this book. My whole reason for this publication is to see people saved and see them SET FREE! I WANT PEOPLE TO BE ALL THAT GOD CREATED THEM TO BE! NOW GO AND WITNESS AND BE USED BY GOD. It's a great feeling being a messenger and a partner in ROUNDING UP THE SHEEP for THE GOOD SHEPHERD.

If you were ALREADY SAVED before you read this book, but GOD TOUCHED YOUR LIFE or the LIFE OF A LOVED ONE, I want you to write me as well. These testimonies are needed to awaken the world to the LIFESTYLE CHANGER and GOOD SHEPHERD – JESUS!

Book TWO will be out soon. Write so you can be notified ahead of time. THE GOOD SHEPHERD LOVES YOU !!!!!!!!!!

Ann,
 What a good friend you have been! We were put together by God & I thank him.
 Rest in the Shepherd's Presence.
Ps. 23:4
 Love-The Shepherd's Rose-
  Kandi
   4-13-05